GreatBooks
Roundtable

Level 1

GreatBooks
Foundation

Copyright © 2010 by The Great Books Foundation

Chicago, Illinois

ISBN 978-1-933147-53-6

6 8 9 7

Printed in the United States of America

Library of Congress Cataloging-in-Publication Data

Great books roundtable. Level 1.
    p. cm.
    ISBN 978-1-933147-53-6 (alk. paper)
    1. Reading (Middle school)–United States. 2. Reading comprehension–
United States. 3. Children–Books and reading–United States. I. Great
Books Foundation (U.S.)
LB1632.G74 2010
372.47–dc22

2009027259

Published and distributed by

THE GREAT BOOKS FOUNDATION
A nonprofit educational organization

35 East Wacker Drive, Suite 400

Chicago, IL 60601

www.greatbooks.org

GreatBooks
Roundtable

Level 1

CONTENTS

PREFACE

Welcome to Great Books Roundtable™! In this reading and discussion program, you will be using a learning method called **Shared Inquiry.**™ In Shared Inquiry, you develop your own **interpretation** of what you read.

Authors do not usually tell us exactly how the parts of a work of literature are connected or spell out why everything in a story happens.

But in good writing, everything fits together and is there for a reason. The parts of the text connect and support each other as the parts of a building do.

Because the parts of a good piece of writing are connected, they help explain one another. Good authors put into their writing the things a reader must know to understand what is happening and why. As you figure out for yourself why the things an author puts in a text are there, you are interpreting what you read. To **interpret** a text is to explain its meaning—what happens in it, and why, and what it is about. Many texts, like those in Great Books programs, support more than one interpretation. When you interpret a text, you are actively seeking out its meaning by asking and exploring questions.

HOW SHARED INQUIRY WORKS

In Shared Inquiry, you read literature that makes you **think and ask questions**.

After reading or listening to the story, poem, or essay, everyone in the group shares questions about it. Some questions can be answered right away. Others will be saved for discussion or other activities.

Everyone then rereads the text and makes notes. Afterward, you all compare your reactions to parts of the text.

You will develop your interpretation of a text most fully in **Shared Inquiry discussion**. During discussion, everyone thinks about the meaning of the text in depth. People sit so everyone can see all the members of the group, and the leader starts discussion with an **interpretive question**—a question that has more than one good answer that can be supported with evidence from the text.

What Shared Inquiry Discussion Looks Like

In a Shared Inquiry discussion, the leader isn't looking for the "right answer." Rather, the leader starts with a question that has more than one good answer based on the text and wants to hear ideas about it.

The leader asks questions to help everyone think more deeply.

In addition to sharing your ideas, you can agree or disagree with someone or ask him a question about his comment.

You can also ask someone to explain her idea a bit more.

At the end of discussion, people will have different answers to the opening question, but everyone will have a better under-standing of the text and the evidence for his or her answer. You may change your answer because of what you hear in discus-sion or hear new evidence to support your original answer.

SHARED INQUIRY DISCUSSION: FIVE GUIDELINES

People of all ages, from kindergartners to adults, participate in Shared Inquiry discussion groups. All participants follow these five guidelines, which help everyone share ideas about the text and learn from one another.

 Read the text twice before participating in the discussion.

 Discuss only the text that everyone has read.

3 Support your ideas with evidence from the text.

4 Listen to other participants, respond to them directly, and ask them questions.

5 Expect the leader to only ask questions, rather than offer opinions or answers.

SHARED INQUIRY DISCUSSION ETIQUETTE

DO

Let other people
talk, and listen to
what they say.

DON'T

Talk over people
and keep others
from speaking.

DO

Speak up! You may
have an idea no one else
has thought of.

DON'T

Be afraid to
share your ideas.

DO

Be willing to think
about new ideas.
Disagree politely.

DON'T

Take it personally
when someone disagrees
with your idea.

DO

Pay attention—it shows
respect for the members
of your group.

DON'T

Distract people or act
as if their ideas aren't
worth hearing.

TYPES OF QUESTIONS

Asking yourself questions is the most important thing you can do while you are reading. When you ask questions, you are helping yourself organize your thoughts about what in the text is interesting, confusing, surprising, shocking, funny, familiar, or sad. You are also preparing to explore the text more deeply the next time you read it. Below are different types of questions you might ask while reading. Notice that it's not always important—or even possible—to answer questions right away.

Factual questions can usually be answered after one thorough reading. The text provides information for a single correct answer.

EXAMPLES: *Where is the girl's mother?* ("Gaston")
Does Raymond win the May Day race?
    ("Raymond's Run")
Why is Jerry's nose always bleeding?
    ("Through the Tunnel")

Background questions must be answered by information outside the text. They might be questions about the historical period in which the text is set, or questions about a character's culture. Sources that can help answer these questions include an encyclopedia, a textbook, the Internet, or a teacher who knows the subject.

EXAMPLES: *Where is Paris?* ("Gaston")
When in history did people start believing in witches?
    ("The Witch Who Came for the Weekend")
Why are the boys holding hands at the beginning?
    ("As the Night the Day")

Evaluative questions go beyond the text and call for the reader's personal opinions. Such questions often ask for a judgment of events or a character's actions.

EXAMPLES: *Is the father a good parent?* ("Gaston")
            Does Frances believe Mr. Addleripe's stories about witches too easily? ("The Witch Who Came for the Weekend")
            Was it a poor decision for Jerry to swim through the tunnel? ("Through the Tunnel")

Speculative questions, like background questions, ask about information that exists outside the text, but readers must guess at or invent the answer using their imagination.

EXAMPLES: *Are the girl's parents divorced?* ("Gaston")
            Why does the old man sell apples? ("The Old Man of the Sea")
            Will Squeaky give up running to coach Raymond? ("Raymond's Run")

Interpretive questions, which get at the text's deeper meaning and themes, are the kind of questions that will be addressed in Shared Inquiry discussion. They have more than one good answer that can be supported with evidence from the text.

EXAMPLES: *Why does the girl squash Gaston?* ("Gaston")
            Why does Mrs. Brennan go on buying two dozen apples even when she asks the old man for less? ("The Old Man of the Sea")
            Why does Kojo decide to confess to breaking the thermometer? ("As the Night the Day")

READING STRATEGIES

Strong readers use certain strategies to help them understand what they read. If you are reading a confusing or puzzling passage, stop and try to figure out which of the reading strategies listed below might help you understand it more clearly. To help you keep track of which strategy you are using, mark your text in the margins with the letters or symbols suggested below:

R   **REREADING**   Go back and reread when you are reading something that is difficult to understand, or when you realize that you haven't been focusing on what you are reading.

?   **ASKING QUESTIONS**   Ask a question about something in the text you find puzzling or confusing.

C   **MAKING CONNECTIONS**   Connect or compare something that happens in the text with something you have experienced or learned yourself.

V   **VISUALIZING**   Create a picture in your head of what is going on in the text. Imagine sights, smells, sounds, and feelings.

!   **NOTING STRONG REACTIONS**   Stop and think about something in the text that causes you to feel a strong reaction (positive *or* negative).

I   **MAKING INFERENCES**   Combine clues in the text with your own ideas to fill in "missing pieces" of the text—places where the author doesn't directly tell you what's going on, but gives you hints by using description, dialogue, or other writing devices.

P   **PREDICTING**   Pause while reading and make a guess, based on your own ideas and the clues in the text, about what might happen next.

If you practice all these strategies, you will eventually begin to use several at a time automatically as you read. Using different comprehension strategies while reading, called *synthesizing*, is how a good reader comes to understand a complex text.

QUICK KEY to Marking Your Text	
R = Rereading	! = Noting strong reactions
? = Asking questions	I = Making inferences
C = Making connections	P = Predicting
V = Visualizing	

FOLLOW-UP QUESTIONS

In Shared Inquiry discussion, the leader isn't the only person who can ask questions. You can respond to your classmates directly by asking them questions yourself. These kinds of questions are called **follow-up questions** because they are useful to ask right after you hear an idea and want to find out more about it. Examples of follow-up questions include:

- Can you say more about what you mean?
- Can you explain that?
- What happened that gave you that idea?
- What part of the story supports your idea?
- Are you agreeing with Amy's answer?
- Why do you agree with what Max said?

Remember: A follow-up question is a compliment. When you ask a follow-up question, you are showing that you are listening and thinking about what others are saying. When someone asks you a follow-up question, that person is displaying interest in your idea.

GASTON

William Saroyan

They were to eat peaches, as planned, after her nap, and now she sat across from the man who would have been a total stranger except that he was in fact her father. They had been together again (although she couldn't quite remember when they had been together before) for almost a hundred years now, or was it only since day before yesterday? Anyhow, they were together again, and he was kind of funny. First, he had the biggest mustache she had ever seen, although to her it was not a mustache at all; it was a lot of red and brown hair under his nose and around the ends of his mouth. Second, he wore a blue and white striped jersey instead of a shirt and tie, and no coat. His arms were covered with the same hair, only it was a little lighter and thinner. He wore blue slacks, but no shoes and socks. He was barefoot, and so was she, of course.

He was at home. She was with him in his home in Paris, if you could call it a home. He was very old, especially for a young man—thirty-six, he had told her; and she was six, just up from sleep on a very hot afternoon in August.

That morning, on a little walk in the neighborhood, she had seen peaches in a box outside a small store and she had stopped to look at them, so he had bought a kilo.

Now the peaches were on a large plate on the card table at which they sat.

There were seven of them, but one of them was flawed. It *looked* as good as the others, almost the size of a tennis ball, nice red fading to light green, but where the stem had been there was now a break that went straight down into the heart of the seed.

He placed the biggest and best-looking peach on the small plate in front of the girl and then took the flawed peach and began to remove the skin. When he had half the skin off the peach he ate that side, neither of them talking, both of them just being there, and not being excited or anything—no plans, that is.

The man held the half-eaten peach and looked down into the cavity, into the open seed. The girl looked, too.

While they were looking, two feelers poked out from the cavity. They were attached to a kind of brown knob-head, which followed the feelers, and then two large legs took a strong grip on the edge of the cavity and hoisted some of the rest of whatever it was out of the seed, and stopped there a moment, as if to look around.

The man studied the seed dweller, and so, of course, did the girl.

The creature paused only a fraction of a second, and then continued to come out of the seed, to walk down the eaten side of the peach to wherever it was going.

The girl had never seen anything like it—a whole big thing made out of brown color, a knob-head, feelers, and a great many legs. It was very active, too. Almost businesslike, you might say.

The man placed the peach back on the plate. The creature moved off the peach onto the surface of the white plate. There it came to a thoughtful stop.

"Who is it?" the girl said.

"Gaston."

"Where does he live?"

"Well, he *used* to live in this peach seed, but now that the peach has been harvested and sold, and I have eaten half of it, it looks as if he's out of house and home."

"Aren't you going to squash him?"

"No, of course not, why should I?"

"He's a bug. He's *ugh*."

"Not at all. He's Gaston, the grand boulevardier."

"Everybody hollers when a bug comes out of an apple, but you don't holler or *anything*."

"Of course not. How would we like it if somebody hollered every time we came out of our house?"

"Why would they?"

"Precisely. So why should we holler at Gaston?"

"He's not the same as us."

"Well, not exactly, but he's the same as a lot of other occupants of peach seeds. Now, the poor fellow hasn't got a home, and there he is with all that pure design and handsome form, and nowhere to go."

"Handsome?"

"Gaston is just about the handsomest of his kind I've ever seen."

"What's he saying?"

"Well, he's a little confused. Now, inside that house of his he had everything in order. Bed here, porch there, etc."

"Show me."

The man picked up the peach, leaving Gaston entirely alone on the white plate. He removed the peeling and ate the rest of the peach.

"Nobody else I know would do that," the girl said. "They'd throw it away."

"I can't imagine why. It's a perfectly good peach." He opened the seed and placed the two sides not far from Gaston. The girl studied the open halves.

"Is *that* where he lives?"

"It's where he used to live. Gaston is out in the world and on his own now. You can see for yourself how comfortable he was in there. He had everything."

"Now what has he got?"

"Not very much, I'm afraid."

"What's he going to do?"

"What are *we* going to do?"

"Well, we're not going to squash him, that's one thing we're *not* going to do," the girl said.

"What *are* we going to do, then?"

"Put him back?"

"Oh, *that* house is finished."

"Well, he can't live in our house, can he?"

"Not happily."

"Can he live in our house *at all?*"

"Well, he could *try,* I suppose. Don't you want a peach?"

"Only if it's a peach with somebody in the seed."

"Well, see if you can find a peach that has an opening at the top, because if you can, that'll be a peach in which you're like-liest to find somebody."

The girl examined each of the peaches on the big plate.

"They're all shut," she said.

"Well, eat one, then."

"No. I want the same kind that you ate, with somebody in the seed."

"Well, to tell you the truth, the peach I ate would be considered a bad peach, so of course stores don't like to sell them. I was sold that one by mistake, most likely. And so now Gaston is without a home, and we've got six perfect peaches to eat."

"I don't want a perfect peach. I want one with people."

"Well, I'll go out and see if I can find one."

"Where will I go?"

"You'll go with me, unless you'd rather stay. I'll only be five minutes."

"If the phone rings, what shall I say?"

"I don't think it'll ring, but if it does, say hello and see who it is."

"If it's my mother, what shall I say?"

"Tell her I've gone to get you a bad peach, and anything else you want to tell her."

"If she wants me to go back, what shall I say?"

"Say yes if you want to go back."

"Do you want me to?"

"Of course not, but the important thing is what you want, not what I want."

"Why is *that* the important thing?"

"Because I want you to be where you want to be."

"I want to be here."

"I'll be right back."

He put on socks and shoes, and a jacket, and went out.

She watched Gaston trying to find out what to do next. Gaston wandered around the plate, but everything seemed wrong and he didn't know what to do or where to go.

The telephone rang and her mother said she was sending the chauffeur to pick her up because there was a little party for somebody's daughter who was also six, and then tomorrow they would fly back to New York.

"Let me speak to your father," she said.

"He's gone to get a peach."

"*One* peach?"

"One with people."

"You haven't been with your father two days and already you *sound* like him."

"There *are* peaches with people in them. I know. I saw one of them come out."

"A *bug*?"

"Not a bug. Gaston."

"*Who*?"

"Gaston the grand something."

"Somebody else gets a peach with a bug in it and throws it away, but not him. He makes up a lot of foolishness about it."

"It's not foolishness."

"All right, all right, don't get angry at me about a horrible peach bug of some kind."

"Gaston is right here, just outside his broken house, and I'm not angry at you."

"You'll have a lot of fun at the party."

"OK."

"We'll have fun flying back to New York, too."

"OK."

"Are you glad you saw your father?"

"Of course I am."

"Is he funny?"

"Yes."

"Is he crazy?"

"Yes. I mean, no. He doesn't holler when he sees a bug crawling out of a peach seed or anything. He just looks at it carefully. But it is just a bug, isn't it really?"

"That's all it is."

"And we'll *have* to squash it?"

"That's right. I can't wait to see you, darling. These two days have been like two years to me. Goodbye."

The girl watched Gaston on the plate, and she actually didn't like him. He was all *ugh*, as he had been in the first place. He didn't have a home anymore and he was wandering around on the white plate and he was silly and wrong and ridiculous and useless and all sorts of other things. She cried a little, but only inside, because long ago she had decided she didn't like crying because if you ever started to cry it seemed as if there was so much to cry about you almost couldn't stop, and she didn't like that at all. The open halves of the peach seed were wrong, too. They were ugly or something. They weren't clean.

The man bought a kilo of peaches but found no flawed peaches among them, so he bought another kilo at another store, and this time there were two that were flawed. He hurried back to his flat and let himself in.

His daughter was in her room, in her best dress.

"My mother phoned," she said, "and she's sending the chauffeur for me because there's another birthday party."

"Another?"

"I mean, there's *always* a lot of them in New York."

"Will the chauffeur bring you back?"

"No. We're flying back to New York tomorrow."

"Oh."

"I liked being in your house."

"I liked having you here."

"Why do you live here?"

"This is my home."

"It's nice, but it's a lot different from our home."

"Yes, I suppose it is."

"It's kind of like Gaston's house."

"Where *is* Gaston?"

"I squashed him."

"Really? Why?"

"Everybody squashes bugs and worms."

"Oh. Well. I found you a peach."

"I don't want a peach anymore."

"OK."

He got her dressed, and he was packing her stuff when the chauffeur arrived. He went down the three flights of stairs with his daughter and the chauffeur, and in the street he was about to hug the girl when he decided he had better not. They shook hands instead, like strangers.

He watched the huge car drive off, then he went around the corner where he took coffee every morning, feeling a little, he thought, like Gaston on the white plate.

THE OLD MAN OF THE SEA

Maeve Brennan

One Thursday afternoon, an ancient man selling apples knocked at the door of our house in Dublin. He appeared to me to be about ninety. His hair was thin and white. His back was stooped, his expression was vague and humble, and he held his hat in one of his hands. His other hand rested on the handle of an enormous basket of apples that stood beside him. My mother, who had opened the door at his knock, stood staring at him. I peered out past her. I was nine. The first question that came into my mind was how did that thin old man carry that big basket of apples—because there was no one in the vicinity, as far as I could see, who might have given him a hand. The second question was how far had he come with his burden. I am sure the same dismayed speculations were in my mother's head, but she had no chance to ask him anything, because as soon as the door began to open he began to talk—to describe his apples and to praise them and to say how cheap they were. After every few words he paused, not so much to catch his breath, it seemed, as to collect his wits and to assure himself that the door was still open and that we were still listening, and, perhaps, to make certain that he himself was still standing where he thought he was. As soon as my mother could with politeness interrupt him, she said hastily that she would take a dozen apples for eating and a dozen for cooking. She got two large bowls from the kitchen, filled them with apples, and paid the old man. She left me to close the door. I watched him shuffle down the tiny tiled path that led to the sidewalk. He closed our gate carefully behind him and started to open the gate next door, but I was quick to tell him that our neighbors were away. He nodded without looking at me, and continued on his way. I hurried into the front sitting room. From the window there, I could see what luck he had at the four other houses that remained for him to visit. By the rapidity with which he retreated from each door, and by the abrupt manner in which he pulled the gates to after him, I judged that he had sold no more apples.

I charged off down to the kitchen. My mother was already peeling the cooking apples. My Uncle Matt, my mother's brother, was standing in the door to the garden, smoking a cigarette. My little sister, Derry, was sitting on a chair and trying to clasp her hands behind its back.

"I suppose you took every apple he had in the basket," my uncle said to my mother.

"Oh, no," I said quickly. "He had most of them left, and he didn't sell any more. We must have been the only people who bought any."

"What did I tell you?" my mother said, not taking her eyes from the apples. "God help him, it would break your heart to see him standing there with his old hat in his hand."

"A half a dozen would have been enough," my uncle said amiably. "Now you've encouraged him, he'll be on your back the rest of your life. Isn't that so, Maeve?"

"Like the Old Man of the Sea," I said, but they paid no attention to me.

"You ought to be ashamed of yourself," my mother said to my uncle, "always thinking the worst of everybody. This is the first time I ever laid eyes on him, and I'd be very much surprised if he ever turns up here again. It's not worth it to him, dragging that big basket around from door to door."

I was thinking of the old man who had attached himself to Sindbad the Sailor. I was thinking how helpless and frail the old man had looked when Sindbad first encountered him, and how, after Sindbad took him on his back to carry him, the old man grew heavier and heavier and stronger and stronger, until, when it was too late, Sindbad began to hate him. It was a story that had fascinated me, especially the description of the old man's cruel, talonlike hands and the way they dug into Sindbad's shoulders.

On the following Thursday, the old apple man again appeared at our door, at the same time in the afternoon. When my mother opened the door, he was standing as before, with his battered hat in his hand and his thin shoulders stooped and the basket of apples beside him, but this time on top of the basket were balanced two large brown paper bags, full of apples. He bent over painfully, lifted the bags, and offered them to my mother, saying something we did not understand. He had to repeat it twice before we caught it. "A dozen of each," he was saying.

My mother started to speak but changed her mind, turned away, got the money, paid him, and took the apples. I stood at the door and stared at him, hoping to catch in his faded eyes a glimpse of the villainy that had possessed the old sinner Sindbad found on the beach, but this old man seemed to have no sight at all. Again I watched him from the front sitting room window, and then I joined my mother in the kitchen.

"He didn't go near any of the other houses," I announced. "I suppose he was afraid they wouldn't buy any."

"I suppose he was," my mother said dismally. "But I didn't want two dozen apples today. The most I would have taken was a half a dozen. And I didn't want to say it the other day with your Uncle Matt here, but he charges more than McRory's." McRory's was the store around the corner where we bought our groceries. "Oh, well," said my mother, "maybe they're better apples." But she left the bags unopened on the kitchen table.

"He was depending on us," I said.

"Oh, I know that very well," my mother said. "I was a fool in the first place, and now I'll never get rid of him. If he turns up next Thursday, I'll take a half a dozen and no more. I'll have the exact money ready."

This resolution cheered her, and she spilled the apples out on the table.

"They are very good apples," she said. "I wonder where he gets them."

"I wonder where he comes from," I said.

"Oh, the poor old Christian," she said. "And he probably has to walk all the way."

"Unless he could find someone to carry him," I said.

"Not with all those apples," she said in surprise.

"He looks very tired," I said, trying to remember if his fingers were talonlike.

"Why wouldn't he look tired?" my mother said. "He's a very old man."

The next Thursday, she had the money ready in her hand when she answered the old man's knock. She hardly had the door open before she spoke.

"I only want a half a dozen apples today," she said clearly, smiling at him. I smiled, too, to show that we meant no harm. He already had the bags in his arms and was lifting them up to her. It was a step down from our front door to the path, so that, although she is a small woman, he appeared smaller than she. She gravely repeated what she had said and shook her head at the bags.

"Just give me a half a dozen," she said, and I could not have told if she was still smiling, because I was staring at the old man. He seemed about to cry. My mother suddenly reached and took the two bags, and hurried away, calling to me to get the money and pay him.

"Now what'll we do?" I asked her when he had gone.

"Oh, it isn't that I mind the apples so much," she said, "but I don't like feeling I *have* to buy them."

"Did you see that his basket is always full up, except for the apples we take?" I said.

"Oh, I suppose he only goes to the ones he's sure of," she said bitterly, "and you can't blame him for that. He's only trying to get along, like everybody else in the world."

The following few Thursdays, we put up no fight, but I did notice that the old man's fingers were not at all talonlike. They were short and stubby, with bulging knuckles.

Then one Thursday afternoon about three months after we had bought the first, fatal two dozen, my mother decided, everything having gone wrong that day, that she would put her foot down once and for all.

"Now look here," she said, "I'm buying no apples from that old fellow today. Even if I wanted them, I wouldn't buy them. Even if he breaks the door down, I won't answer it."

Derry and I exchanged a glance of anticipation. We were going to pretend we weren't in. We had done that before when unwanted callers came, and we enjoyed it very much. We liked keeping rigidly quiet, listening to the futile knocking at the front door, and we especially enjoyed having our mother at our mercy for those few minutes, because we all felt sure that the least squeak we made, no matter where we were in the house, would betray us to the straining ears outside. Then there was always the sense of triumph when at last we heard our little gate clang shut again and knew that we had defeated our enemy. This time, however, there was an extra suspense that we could not have explained. We were all in the kitchen when the old man's knock came. Our kitchen was separated from our front door only by the length of a small, narrow hall, so we shut the kitchen door. We heard the first knock, and then the second, and then the third. Finally, the old man knocked several times more in rapid succession. Derry and I began to reel around, giggling helplessly, and my mother gave us a reproachful look. She was distressed anyway.

A familiar scratching noise came to our ears, and we gazed at one another, aghast.

"He must have got in somehow," my mother said in a fearful whisper.

I opened the kitchen door very gradually. "He's got his hand in the letter box," I whispered over my shoulder to the others.

In the middle of the front door there was a wide slot through which the postman pushed letters and papers so that they fell inside on the hall floor. On the outside, the slot was protected by a brass flap, and the old man had lifted this and was trying to peer into the hall. We knew very well that the slot gave only a limited and indistinct view of the hall, but we were unreasonably startled to realize that he had found an opening in the house. Suddenly he began to shout through the slot.

"He's roaring mad!" Derry whispered. "He'll kill us all."

"Can you make out what he's saying?" asked my mother, who was appalled.

"He's saying, 'Apple, apple, apple,'" I said.

Derry and I collapsed into hysterical mirth. My mother bundled us out into the garden and came out herself.

"Have you no heart?" she said. "To laugh at an unfortunate old man who probably never gets enough to eat!"

"Now we're really not in," I said, "because we're out in the garden."

Derry joined me in screeches of laughter.

"If I thought he could hear you," my mother said fiercely to us, "I'd murder you both."

"Well, it's too late to answer the door now," she added. "I couldn't face him after this. I'll make it up to him next week."

There was sudden silence—no knocking, no shouting.

"He's gone away," my mother said, in a tone of guilty relief.

At that moment, the tousled head and avid eyes of the woman next door appeared over the wall that separated our garden from hers. "Mrs. Brennan!" she shouted. She had a powerful voice. "There's an old fellow outside with apples for you. He says he's been at your door for a half an hour. He says he comes regularly and he knows you're depending on him. I told him you were in the garden. He must be back around at your door by now. There he is."

There he was. The knocking had started again.

"Oh, God forgive me!" my mother cried. "That old villain! He must have known I was hiding from him."

"What are you hiding for?" our neighbor shrieked. "Do you owe him?"

"Oh, no," my mother said indignantly, "but I don't want any apples."

"Well, why don't you just tell him to go about his business?"

"I will, of course. That's what I'm going to do."

"Just give him a piece of your mind for making a nuisance of himself and shut the door in his face," commanded our neighbor, with relish.

My mother went into our kitchen, took her purse in her hand, and marched to the door, with Derry and me following. The old man was a pitiful sight. He had forgotten to take off his hat, and his eyes glittered, whether with anguish or with anger it would have been hard to say. He pushed the two bags of apples rudely into my mother's arms without looking at her. She opened her purse to pay him and gave a cry of distress: "Didn't I go and pay the grocer only an hour ago, and I'm fourpence short!" She handed him the money and showed him that it left her purse empty. "It's all I have in the house at the minute," she said.

He grabbed the money, counted it, and gave her back a dreadful look of contempt. Then he lifted his enormous basket, which was, as always, full to the brim, and turned his back on us. This time, we all stood in the front sitting room window and watched him. He didn't close our gate, and he scuttled slowly off down the street as though he couldn't get away from us fast enough.

"First, he thought we were making fun of him," my mother said, "and now he thinks I was trying to bargain with him. He might have known I'd make it up to him the next time."

She, who never tried to bargain with anybody in her life, was filled with shame.

"Next week, we'll have the door open for him before he knocks," I said.

But the following week there was no sign of the old man, and he never came near us again, although, filled with remorse, we watched for him. One afternoon, my Uncle Matt dropped around to see us, and my mother, in a confiding mood, told him the whole story.

"Well, I could have told you," he said, grinning.

"It wasn't so much the apples, you know," my mother said.

"Oh, no," said my uncle. "You'd have liked him to come to your door and ask straight out for money, like the rest of your beggars."

My mother was noted for her inability to refuse food, clothes, or money to anybody who came to the door.

"How many times must I tell you not to call them beggars," she said angrily now to my uncle. "They're just unfortunate, and I wouldn't be so quick to laugh at them if I were you."

"Well, you're well rid of *him*," my uncle said. "And I may as well tell you now that I saw him strolling down O'Connell Street the other morning wearing a suit of clothes that I couldn't afford to buy, and not an apple in sight. There's your poor old man for you."

"Now how did you know it was him?" my mother cried skeptically. "You never saw him at all."

"Wasn't I here the first time he came to the door? I was standing in the middle of the kitchen, and you had the hall door wide open. Of course I saw him."

"Well, you're making all that up about seeing him on O'Connell Street."

"I saw him, and I passed close enough to touch him. He had his married daughter from Drumcondra with him."

"And how do you know she was his married daughter from Drumcondra, may I ask?"

"Oh, you couldn't mistake *her*," my uncle said airily. "I knew her by the way she was wearing her hat."

"That tongue of yours, Matt," my mother said. "I never know whether to believe you or not."

For my part, I believed every word my uncle said.

THROUGH THE TUNNEL

Doris Lessing

Going to the shore on the first morning of the vacation, the young English boy stopped at a turning of the path and looked down at a wild and rocky bay, and then over to the crowded beach he knew so well from other years. His mother walked on in front of him, carrying a bright striped bag in one hand. Her other arm, swinging loose, was very white in the sun. The boy watched that white naked arm, and turned his eyes, which had a frown behind them, towards the bay and back again to his mother. When she felt he was not with her, she swung around. "Oh, there you are, Jerry!" she said. She looked impatient, then smiled. "Why, darling, would you rather not come with me? Would you rather—" She frowned, conscientiously worrying over what amusements he might secretly be longing for, which she had been too busy or too careless to imagine. He was very familiar with that anxious, apologetic smile. Contrition sent him running after her. And yet, as he ran, he looked back over his shoulder at the wild bay;

and all morning, as he played on the safe beach, he was thinking of it.

Next morning, when it was time for the routine of swimming and sunbathing, his mother said, "Are you tired of the usual beach, Jerry? Would you like to go somewhere else?"

"Oh, no!" he said quickly, smiling at her out of that unfailing impulse of contrition—a sort of chivalry. Yet, walking down the path with her, he blurted out, "I'd like to go and have a look at those rocks down there."

She gave the idea her attention. It was a wild-looking place, and there was no one there; but she said, "Of course, Jerry. When you've had enough, come to the big beach. Or just go straight back to the villa, if you like." She walked away, that bare arm, now slightly reddened from yesterday's sun, swinging. And he almost ran after her again, feeling it unbearable that she should go by herself, but he did not.

She was thinking, Of course he's old enough to be safe without me. Have I been keeping him too close? He mustn't feel he ought to be with me. I must be careful.

He was an only child, eleven years old. She was a widow. She was determined to be neither possessive nor lacking in devotion. She went worrying off to her beach.

As for Jerry, once he saw that his mother had gained her beach, he began the steep descent to the bay. From where he was, high up among red-brown rocks, it was a scoop of moving blueish green fringed with white. As he went lower, he saw that it spread among small promontories and inlets of rough, sharp rock, and the crisping, lapping surface showed stains of purple and darker blue. Finally, as he ran sliding and scraping down the last few yards, he saw an edge of white surf and the shallow, luminous movement of water over white sand, and, beyond that, a solid, heavy blue.

He ran straight into the water and began swimming. He was a good swimmer. He went out fast over the gleaming sand, over a middle region where rocks lay like discoloured monsters under the surface, and then he was in the real sea—a warm sea where irregular cold currents from the deep water shocked his limbs.

When he was so far out that he could look back not only on the little bay but past the promontory that was between it and the big beach, he floated on the buoyant surface and looked for his mother. There she was, a speck of yellow under an umbrella that looked like a slice of orange peel. He swam back to shore, relieved at being sure she was there, but all at once very lonely.

On the edge of a small cape that marked the side of the bay away from the promontory was a loose scatter of rocks. Above them, some boys were stripping off their clothes. They came running, naked, down to the rocks. The English boy swam towards them, but kept his distance at a stone's throw. They were of that coast; all of them were burned smooth dark brown and speaking a language he did not understand. To be with them, of them, was a craving that filled his whole body. He swam a little closer; they turned and watched him with narrowed, alert dark eyes. Then one smiled and waved. It was enough. In a minute, he had swum in and was on the rocks beside them, smiling with a desperate, nervous supplication. They shouted cheerful greetings at him; and then, as he preserved his nervous, uncomprehending smile, they understood that he was a foreigner strayed from his own beach, and they proceeded to forget him. But he was happy. He was with them.

They began diving again and again from a high point into a well of blue sea between rough, pointed rocks. After they had dived and come up, they swam around, hauled themselves up, and waited their turn to dive again. They were big boys—men, to Jerry. He dived, and they watched him; and when he swam around to take his place, they made way for him. He felt he was accepted and he dived again, carefully, proud of himself.

Soon the biggest of the boys poised himself, shot down into the water, and did not come up. The others stood about, watching. Jerry, after waiting for the sleek brown head to appear, let out a yell of warning; they looked at him idly and turned their eyes back towards the water. After a long time, the boy came up on the other side of a big dark rock, letting the air out of his lungs in a sputtering gasp and a shout of triumph. Immediately the rest of them dived in. One moment, the morning seemed full of chattering boys; the next, the air and the surface of the water were empty. But through the heavy blue, dark shapes could be seen moving and groping.

Jerry dived, shot past the school of underwater swimmers, saw a black wall of rock looming at him, touched it, and bobbed up at once to the surface, where the wall was a low barrier he could see across. There was no one visible; under him, in the water, the dim shapes of the swimmers had disappeared. Then one, and then another of the boys came up on the far side of the barrier of rock, and he understood that they had swum through some gap or hole in it. He plunged down again. He could see nothing through the stinging salt water but the blank rock. When he came up the boys were all on the diving rock, preparing to attempt the feat again. And now, in a panic of failure, he yelled up, in English, "Look at me! Look!" and he began splashing and kicking in the water like a foolish dog.

They looked down gravely, frowning. He knew the frown. At moments of failure, when he clowned to claim his mother's attention, it was with just this grave, embarrassed inspection that she rewarded him. Through his hot shame, feeling the pleading grin on his face like a scar that he could never remove, he looked up at the group of big brown boys on the rock and shouted *"Bonjour! Merci! Au revoir! Monsieur, monsieur!"* while he hooked his fingers round his ears and waggled them.

Water surged into his mouth; he choked, sank, came up. The rock, lately weighted with boys, seemed to rear up out of the water as their weight was removed. They were flying down past him now, into the water; the air was full of falling bodies. Then the rock was empty in the hot sunlight. He counted one, two, three . . .

At fifty, he was terrified. They must all be drowning beneath him, in the watery caves of the rock! At a hundred, he stared around him at the empty hillside, wondering if he should yell for help. He counted faster, faster, to hurry them up, to bring them to the surface quickly, to drown them quickly—anything rather than the terror of counting on and on into the blue emptiness of the morning. And then, at a hundred and sixty, the water beyond the rock was full of boys blowing like brown whales. They swam back to the shore without a look at him.

He climbed back to the diving rock and sat down, feeling the hot roughness of it under his thighs. The boys were gathering up their bits of clothing and running off along the shore to another promontory. They were leaving to get away from him. He cried openly, fists in his eyes. There was no one to see him, and he cried himself out.

It seemed to him that a long time had passed, and he swam out to where he could see his mother. Yes, she was still there, a yellow spot under an orange umbrella. He swam back to the big rock, climbed up, and dived into the blue pool among the fanged and angry boulders. Down he went, until he touched the wall of rock again. But the salt was so painful in his eyes that he could not see.

He came to the surface, swam to shore, and went back to the villa to wait for his mother. Soon she walked slowly up the path, swinging her striped bag, the flushed, naked arm dangling beside her. "I want some swimming goggles," he panted, defiant and beseeching.

She gave him a patient, inquisitive look as she said casually, "Well, of course, darling."

But now, now, now! He must have them this minute, and no other time. He nagged and pestered until she went with him to a shop. As soon as she had bought the goggles, he grabbed them from her hand as if she were going to claim them for herself, and was off, running down the steep path to the bay.

Jerry swam out to the big barrier rock, adjusted the goggles, and dived. The impact of the water broke the rubber-enclosed vacuum, and the goggles came loose. He understood that he must swim down to the base of the rock from the surface of the water. He fixed the goggles tight and firm, filled his lungs, and floated, face down, on the water. Now he could see. It was as if he had eyes of a different kind—fish eyes that showed everything clear and delicate and wavering in the bright water.

Under him, six or seven feet down, was a floor of perfectly clean, shining white sand, rippled firm and hard by the tides. Two greyish shapes steered there, like long, rounded pieces of wood or slate. They were fish. He saw them nose towards each other, poise motionless, make a dart forward, swerve off, and come around again. It was like a water dance. A few inches above them the water sparkled as if sequins were dropping through it. Fish again—myriads of minute fish, the length of his fingernail—were drifting through the water, and in a moment he could feel the innumerable tiny touches of them against his limbs. It was like swimming in flaked silver. The great rock the big boys had swum through rose sheer out of the

28

white sand—black, tufted lightly with greenish weed. He could see no gap in it. He swam down to its base.

Again and again he rose, took a big chestful of air, and went down. Again and again he groped over the surface of the rock, feeling it, almost hugging it in the desperate need to find the entrance. And then, once, while he was clinging to the black wall, his knees came up and he shot his feet out forward and they met no obstacle. He had found the hole.

He gained the surface, clambered about the stones that littered the barrier rock until he found a big one, and, with this in his arms, let himself down over the side of the rock. He dropped, with the weight, straight to the sandy floor. Clinging tight to the anchor of stone, he lay on his side and looked in under the dark shelf at the place where his feet had gone. He could see the hole. It was an irregular, dark gap; but he could not see deep into it. He let go of his anchor, clung with his hands to the edges of the hole, and tried to push himself in.

He got his head in, found his shoulders jammed, moved them in sidewise, and was inside as far as his waist. He could see nothing ahead. Something soft and clammy touched his mouth; he saw a dark frond moving against the greyish rock, and panic filled him. He thought of octopuses, of clinging weed. He pushed himself out backward and caught a glimpse, as he retreated, of a harmless tentacle of seaweed drifting in the mouth of the tunnel. But it was enough. He reached the sunlight, swam to shore, and lay on the diving rock. He looked down into the blue well of water. He knew he must find his way through that cave, or hole, or tunnel, and out the other side.

First, he thought, he must learn to control his breathing. He let himself down into the water with another big stone in his arms, so that he could lie effortlessly on the bottom of the sea. He counted. One, two, three. He counted steadily. He could

hear the movement of blood in his chest. Fifty-one, fifty-two
. . . His chest was hurting. He let go of the rock and went up
into the air. He saw that the sun was low. He rushed to the villa
and found his mother at her supper. She said only, "Did you
enjoy yourself?" and he said, "Yes."

All night the boy dreamed of the water-filled cave in the
rock, and as soon as breakfast was over he went to the bay.

That night, his nose bled badly. For hours he had been
underwater, learning to hold his breath, and now he felt weak
and dizzy. His mother said, "I shouldn't overdo things, darling,
if I were you."

That day and the next, Jerry exercised his lungs as if everything, the whole of his life, all that he would become, depended
upon it. Again his nose bled at night, and his mother insisted
on his coming with her the next day. It was a torment to him
to waste a day of his careful self-training, but he stayed with her
on that other beach, which now seemed a place for small children, a place where his mother might lie safe in the sun. It was
not his beach.

He did not ask for permission, on the following day, to go
to his beach. He went, before his mother could consider the
complicated rights and wrongs of the matter. A day's rest, he
discovered, had improved his count by ten. The big boys had
made the passage while he counted a hundred and sixty. He had
been counting fast, in his fright. Probably now, if he tried, he
could get through that long tunnel, but he was not going to try
yet. A curious, most unchildlike persistence, a controlled impa-
tience, made him wait. In the meantime, he lay underwater on
the white sand, littered now by stones he had brought down
from the upper air, and studied the entrance to the tunnel. He
knew every jut and corner of it, as far as it was possible to see. It
was as if he already felt its sharpness about his shoulders.

He sat by the clock in the villa, when his mother was not near, and checked his time. He was incredulous and then proud to find he could hold his breath without strain for two minutes. The words *two minutes*, authorised by the clock, brought close the adventure that was so necessary to him.

In another four days, his mother said casually one morning, they must go home. On the day before they left, he would do it. He would do it if it killed him, he said defiantly to himself. But two days before they were to leave—a day of triumph when he increased his count by fifteen—his nose bled so badly that he turned dizzy and had to lie limply over the big rock like a bit of seaweed, watching the thick red blood flow onto the rock and trickle slowly down to the sea. He was frightened. Supposing he turned dizzy in the tunnel? Supposing he died there, trapped? Supposing—his head went around, in the hot sun, and he almost gave up. He thought he would return to the house and lie down, and next summer, perhaps, when he had another year's growth in him—*then* he would go through the hole.

But even after he had made the decision, or thought he had, he found himself sitting up on the rock and looking down into the water; and he knew that now, this moment, when his nose had only just stopped bleeding, when his head was still sore and throbbing—this was the moment when he would try. If he did not do it now, he never would. He was trembling with fear that he would not go; and he was trembling with horror at the long, long tunnel under the rock, under the sea. Even in the open sunlight, the barrier rock seemed very wide and very heavy; tons of rock pressed down on where he would go. If he died there, he would lie until one day—perhaps not before next year—those big boys would swim into it and find it blocked.

He put on his goggles, fitted them tight, tested the vacuum. His hands were shaking. Then he chose the biggest stone he

31

could carry and slipped over the edge of the rock until half of him was in the cool enclosing water and half in the hot sun. He looked up once at the empty sky, filled his lungs once, twice, and then sank fast to the bottom with the stone. He let it go and began to count. He took the edges of the hole in his hands and drew himself into it, wriggling his shoulders in sidewise as he remembered he must, kicking himself along with his feet.

Soon he was clear inside. He was in a small rock-bound hole filled with yellowish grey water. The water was pushing him up against the roof. The roof was sharp and pained his back. He pulled himself along with his hands—fast, fast—and used his legs as levers. His head knocked against something; a sharp pain dizzied him. Fifty, fifty-one, fifty-two . . . He was without light, and the water seemed to press upon him with the weight of rock. Seventy-one, seventy-two . . . There was no strain on his lungs. He felt like an inflated balloon, his lungs were so light and easy, but his head was pulsing.

He was being continually pressed against the sharp roof, which felt slimy as well as sharp. Again he thought of octopuses, and wondered if the tunnel might be filled with weed that could tangle him. He gave himself a panicky, convulsive kick forward, ducked his head, and swam. His feet and hands moved freely, as if in open water. The hole must have widened out. He thought he must be swimming fast, and he was frightened of banging his head if the tunnel narrowed.

A hundred, a hundred and one . . . The water paled. Victory filled him. His lungs were beginning to hurt. A few more strokes and he would be out. He was counting wildly; he said a hundred and fifteen, and then, a long time later, a hundred and fifteen again. The water was a clear jewel-green all around him. Then he saw, above his head, a crack running up through the rock. Sunlight was falling through it, showing the clean, dark rock of the tunnel, a single mussel shell, and darkness ahead.

He was at the end of what he could do. He looked up at the crack as if it were filled with air and not water, as if he could put his mouth to it to draw in air. A hundred and fifteen, he heard himself say inside his head—but he had said that long ago. He must go on into the blackness ahead, or he would drown. His head was swelling, his lungs cracking. A hundred and fifteen, a hundred and fifteen pounded through his head, and he feebly clutched at rocks in the dark, pulling himself forward, leaving the brief space of sunlit water behind. He felt he was dying. He was no longer quite conscious. He struggled on in the darkness between lapses into unconsciousness. An immense, swelling pain filled his head, and then the darkness cracked with an explosion of green light. His hands, groping forward, met nothing; and his feet, kicking back, propelled him out into the open sea.

He drifted to the surface, his face turned up to the air. He was gasping like a fish. He felt he would sink now and drown; he could not swim the few feet back to the rock. Then he was clutching it and pulling himself up onto it. He lay face down, gasping. He could see nothing but a red-veined, clotted dark. His eyes must have burst, he thought; they were full of blood. He tore off his goggles and a gout of blood went into the sea. His nose was bleeding, and the blood had filled the goggles.

He scooped up handfuls of water from the cool, salty sea, to splash on his face, and did not know whether it was blood or salt water he tasted. After a time, his heart quieted, his eyes cleared, and he sat up. He could see the local boys diving and playing half a mile away. He did not want them. He wanted nothing but to get back home and lie down.

In a short while, Jerry swam to shore and climbed slowly up the path to the villa. He flung himself on his bed and slept, waking at the sound of feet on the path outside. His mother was coming back. He rushed to the bathroom, thinking she must not see his face with bloodstains, or tearstains, on it. He came out of the bathroom and met her as she walked into the villa, smiling, her eyes lighting up.

"Have a nice morning?" she asked, laying her hand on his warm brown shoulder a moment.

"Oh, yes, thank you," he said.

"You look a bit pale." And then, sharp and anxious, "How did you bang your head?"

"Oh, just banged it," he told her.

She looked at him closely. He was strained; his eyes were glazed-looking. She was worried. And then she said to herself, Oh, don't fuss! Nothing can happen. He can swim like a fish.

They sat down to lunch together.

"Mummy," he said, "I can stay underwater for two minutes— three minutes, at least." It came bursting out of him.

"Can you, darling?" she said. "Well, I shouldn't overdo it. I don't think you ought to swim anymore today."

She was ready for a battle of wills, but he gave in at once. It was no longer of the least importance to go to the bay.

RAYMOND'S RUN

Toni Cade Bambara

I don't have much work to do around the house like some girls. My mother does that. And I don't have to earn my pocket money by hustling; George runs errands for the big boys and sells Christmas cards. And anything else that's got to get done, my father does. All I have to do in life is mind my brother Raymond, which is enough.

Sometimes I slip and say my little brother Raymond. But as any fool can see he's much bigger and he's older too. But a lot of people call him my little brother cause he needs looking after cause he's not quite right. And a lot of smart mouths got lots to say about that too, especially when George was minding him. But now, if anybody has anything to say to Raymond, anything to say about his big head, they have to come by me. And I don't play the dozens or believe in standing around with somebody in my face doing a lot of talking. I much rather just knock you down and take my chances even if I am a little girl with skinny arms and a squeaky voice, which is how I got the name Squeaky. And if things get too rough, I run. And as anybody can tell you, I'm the fastest thing on two feet.

There is no track meet that I don't win the first-place medal. I used to win the twenty-yard dash when I was a little kid in kindergarten. Nowadays, it's the fifty-yard dash. And tomorrow I'm subject to run the quarter-meter relay all by myself and come in first, second, and third. The big kids call me Mercury cause I'm the swiftest thing in the neighborhood. Everybody knows that—except two people who know better, my father and me. He can beat me to Amsterdam Avenue with me having a two-fire-hydrant head start and him running with his hands in his pockets and whistling. But that's private information. Cause can you imagine some thirty-five-year-old man stuffing himself into PAL shorts to race little kids? So as far as everyone's concerned, I'm the fastest and that goes for Gretchen, too, who has put out the tale that she is going to win the first-place medal this year. Ridiculous. In the second place, she's got short legs. In the third place, she's got freckles. In the first place, no one can beat me and that's all there is to it.

I'm standing on the corner admiring the weather and about to take a stroll down Broadway so I can practice my breathing exercises, and I've got Raymond walking on the inside close to the buildings, cause he's subject to fits of fantasy and starts thinking he's a circus performer and that the curb is a tightrope strung high in the air. And sometimes after a rain he likes to step down off his tightrope right into the gutter and slosh around getting his shoes and cuffs wet. Then I get hit when I get home. Or sometimes if you don't watch him he'll dash across traffic to the island in the middle of Broadway and give the pigeons a fit. Then I have to go behind him apologizing to all the old people sitting around trying to get some sun and getting all upset with the pigeons fluttering around them, scattering their newspapers and upsetting the wax-paper lunches in their laps. So I keep Raymond on the inside of me, and he plays like he's driving a stagecoach which is OK by me so long as he doesn't run me over or interrupt my breathing exercises, which I have to do on account of I'm serious about my running, and I don't care who knows it.

Now some people like to act like things come easy to them, won't let on that they practice. Not me. I'll high-prance down 34th Street like a rodeo pony to keep my knees strong even if it does get my mother uptight so that she walks ahead like she's not with me, don't know me, is all by herself on a shopping trip, and I am somebody else's crazy child. Now you take Cynthia Procter for instance. She's just the opposite. If there's a test tomorrow, she'll say something like, "Oh, I guess I'll play handball this afternoon and watch television tonight," just to let you know she ain't thinking about the test. Or like last week when she won the spelling bee for the millionth time, "A good thing you got 'receive,' Squeaky, cause I would have got it wrong. I completely forgot about the spelling bee." And she'll clutch the lace on her blouse like it was a narrow escape. Oh, brother. But of course when I pass her house on my early morning trots around the block, she is practicing the scales on the piano over and over and over and over. Then in music class she always lets herself get bumped around so she falls accidently on purpose onto the piano stool and is so surprised to find herself sitting there that she decides just for fun to try out the ole keys. And what do you know—Chopin's waltzes just spring out of her fingertips and she's the most surprised thing in the world. A regular prodigy. I could kill people like that. I stay up all night studying the words for the spelling bee. And you can see me any time of day practicing running. I never walk if I can trot, and shame on Raymond if he can't keep up. But of course he does, cause if he hangs back someone's liable to walk up to him and get smart, or take his allowance from him, or ask him where he got that great big pumpkin head. People are so stupid sometimes.

So I'm strolling down Broadway breathing out and breathing in on counts of seven, which is my lucky number, and here comes Gretchen and her sidekicks: Mary Louise, who used to be a friend of mine when she first moved to Harlem from Baltimore and got beat up by everybody till I took up for her on account of her mother and my mother used to sing in the same choir when they were young girls, but people ain't grateful, so now she hangs out with the new girl Gretchen and talks about me like a dog; and Rosie, who is as fat as I am skinny and has a big mouth where Raymond is concerned and is too stupid to know that there is not a big deal of difference between herself and Raymond and that she can't afford to throw stones. So they are steady coming up Broadway and I see right away that it's going to be one of those Dodge City scenes cause the street ain't that big and they're close to the buildings just as we are. First I think I'll step into the candy store and look over the new comics and let them pass. But that's chicken and I've got a reputation to consider. So then I think I'll just walk straight on through them or even over them if necessary. But as they get to me, they slow down. I'm ready to fight, cause like I said I don't feature a whole lot of chitchat, I much prefer to just knock you down right from the jump and save everybody a lotta precious time.

"You signing up for the May Day races?" smiles Mary Louise, only it's not a smile at all. A dumb question like that doesn't deserve an answer. Besides, there's just me and Gretchen standing there really, so no use wasting my breath talking to shadows.

"I don't think you're going to win this time," says Rosie, trying to signify with her hands on her hips all salty, completely forgetting that I have whupped her behind many times for less salt than that.

"I always win cause I'm the best," I say straight at Gretchen who is, as far as I'm concerned, the only one talking in this ventriloquist-dummy routine. Gretchen smiles, but it's not a smile, and I'm thinking that girls never really smile at each other because they don't know how and don't want to know how and there's probably no one to teach us how, cause grown-up girls don't know either. Then they all look at Raymond who has just brought his mule team to a standstill. And they're about to see what trouble they can get into through him.

"What grade you in now, Raymond?"

"You got anything to say to my brother, you say it to me, Mary Louise Williams of Raggedy Town, Baltimore."

"What are you, his mother?" sasses Rosie.

"That's right, Fatso. And the next word out of anybody and I'll be *their* mother too." So they just stand there and Gretchen shifts from one leg to the other and so do they. Then Gretchen puts her hands on her hips and is about to say something with her freckle-face self but doesn't. Then she walks around me looking me up and down but keeps walking up Broadway, and her sidekicks follow her. So me and Raymond smile at each other and he says, "Gidyap" to his team and I continue with my breathing exercises, strolling down Broadway toward the ice man on 145th with not a care in the world cause I am Miss Quicksilver herself.

I take my time getting to the park on May Day because the track meet is the last thing on the program. The biggest thing on the program is the Maypole dancing, which I can do without, thank you, even if my mother thinks it's a shame I

41

don't take part and act like a girl for a change. You'd think my mother'd be grateful not to have to make me a white organdy dress with a big satin sash and buy me new white baby-doll shoes that can't be taken out of the box till the big day. You'd think she'd be glad her daughter ain't out there prancing around a Maypole getting the new clothes all dirty and sweaty and trying to act like a fairy or a flower or whatever you're supposed to be when you should be trying to be yourself, whatever that is, which is, as far as I am concerned, a poor Black girl who really can't afford to buy shoes and a new dress you only wear once a lifetime cause it won't fit next year.

I was once a strawberry in a Hansel and Gretel pageant when I was in nursery school and didn't have no better sense than to dance on tiptoe with my arms in a circle over my head doing umbrella steps and being a perfect fool just so my mother and father could come dressed up and clap. You'd think they'd know better than to encourage that kind of nonsense. I am not a strawberry. I do not dance on my toes. I run. That is what I am all about. So I always come late to the May Day program, just in time to get my number pinned on and lay in the grass till they announce the fifty-yard dash.

I put Raymond in the little swings, which is a tight squeeze this year and will be impossible next year. Then I look around for Mr. Pearson, who pins the numbers on. I'm really looking for Gretchen if you want to know the truth, but she's not around. The park is jam-packed. Parents in hats and corsages and breast-pocket handkerchiefs peeking up. Kids in white dresses and light-blue suits. The parkees unfolding chairs and chasing the rowdy kids from Lenox as if they had no right to be there. The big guys with their caps on backwards, leaning against the fence swirling the basketballs on the tips of their fingers, waiting for all these crazy people to clear out the park so they can play. Most of the kids in my class are carrying bass drums and glockenspiels and flutes. You'd think they'd put in a few bongos or something for real like that.

Then here comes Mr. Pearson with his clipboard and his cards and pencils and whistles and safety pins and fifty million other things he's always dropping all over the place with his clumsy self. He sticks out in a crowd because he's on stilts. We used to call him Jack and the Beanstalk to get him mad. But I'm the only one that can outrun him and get away, and I'm too grown for that silliness now.

"Well, Squeaky," he says, checking my name off the list and handing me number seven and two pins. And I'm thinking he's got no right to call me Squeaky, if I can't call him Beanstalk.

"Hazel Elizabeth Deborah Parker," I correct him and tell him to write it down on his board.

"Well, Hazel Elizabeth Deborah Parker, going to give someone else a break this year?" I squint at him real hard to see if he is seriously thinking I should lose the race on purpose just to give someone else a break. "Only six girls running this time," he continues, shaking his head sadly like it's my fault all of New York didn't turn out in sneakers. "That new girl should give you a run for your money." He looks around the park for Gretchen like a periscope in a submarine movie. "Wouldn't it be a nice gesture if you were . . . to ahhh . . . "

I give him such a look he couldn't finish putting that idea into words. Grownups got a lot of nerve sometimes. I pin number seven to myself and stomp away, I'm so burnt. And I go straight for the track and stretch out on the grass while the band winds up with "Oh, the Monkey Wrapped His Tail Around the Flag Pole," which my teacher calls by some other name. The man on the loudspeaker is calling everyone over to the track and I'm on my back looking at the sky, trying to pretend I'm in the country, but I can't, because even grass in the city feels hard as sidewalk, and there's just no pretending you are anywhere but in a "concrete jungle" as my grandfather says.

The twenty-yard dash takes all of two minutes cause most of the little kids don't know no better than to run off the track or run the wrong way or run smack into the fence and fall down and cry. One little kid, though, has got the good sense to run straight for the white ribbon up ahead so he wins. Then the second graders line up for the thirty-yard dash and I don't even bother to turn my head to watch cause Raphael Perez always wins. He wins before he even begins by psyching the runners, telling them they're going to trip on their shoelaces and fall on their faces or lose their shorts or something, which he doesn't really have to do since he is very fast, almost as fast as I am. After that is the forty-yard dash which I use to run when I was in first grade. Raymond is hollering from the swings cause he knows I'm about to do my thing cause the man on the loud-speaker has just announced the fifty-yard dash, although he might just as well be giving a recipe for angel food cake cause you can hardly make out what he's sayin for the static. I get up and slip off my sweat pants and then I see Gretchen standing at the starting line, kicking her legs out like a pro. Then as I get into place I see that ole Raymond is on line on the other side of the fence, bending down with his fingers on the ground just like he knew what he was doing. I was going to yell at him but then I didn't. It burns up your energy to holler.

Every time, just before I take off in a race, I always feel like I'm in a dream, the kind of dream you have when you're sick with fever and feel all hot and weightless. I dream I'm flying over a sandy beach in the early morning sun, kissing the leaves of the trees as I fly by. And there's always the smell of apples, just like in the country when I was little and used to think

I was a choo-choo train, running through the fields of corn and chugging up the hill to the orchard. And all the time I'm dreaming this, I get lighter and lighter until I'm flying over the beach again, getting blown through the sky like a feather that weighs nothing at all. But once I spread my fingers in the dirt and crouch over the Get on Your Mark, the dream goes and I am solid again and am telling myself, Squeaky you must win, you must win, you are the fastest thing in the world, you can even beat your father up Amsterdam if you really try. And then I feel my weight coming back just behind my knees then down to my feet then into the earth and the pistol shot explodes in my blood and I am off and weightless again, flying past the other runners, my arms pumping up and down and the whole world is quiet except for the crunch as I zoom over the gravel in the track. I glance to my left and there is no one. To the right, a blurred Gretchen, who's got her chin jutting out as if it would win the race all by itself. And on the other side of the fence is Raymond with his arms down to his side and the palms tucked up behind him, running in his very own style, and it's the first time I ever saw that and I almost stop to watch my brother Raymond on his first run. But the white ribbon is bouncing toward me and I tear past it, racing into the distance till my feet with a mind of their own start digging up footfuls of dirt and brake me short. Then all the kids standing on the side pile on me, banging me on the back and slapping my head with their May Day programs, for I have won again and everybody on 151st Street can walk tall for another year.

"In first place . . ." the man on the loudspeaker is clear as a bell now. But then he pauses and the loudspeaker starts to whine. Then static. And I lean down to catch my breath and here comes Gretchen walking back, for she's overshot the finish line too, huffing and puffing with her hands on her hips taking it slow, breathing in steady time like a real pro and I sort of like her a little for the first time. "In first place . . ." and then three or four voices get all mixed up on the loudspeaker and I dig my sneaker into the grass and stare at Gretchen who's staring back, we both wondering just who did win. I can hear old Beanstalk arguing with the man on the loudspeaker and then a few others running their mouths about what the stopwatches say. Then I hear Raymond yanking at the fence to call me and I wave to shush him, but he keeps rattling the fence like a gorilla in a cage like in them gorilla movies, but then like a dancer or something he starts climbing up nice and easy but very fast. And it occurs to me, watching how smoothly he climbs hand over hand and remembering how he looked running with his arms down to his side and with the wind pulling his mouth back and his teeth showing and all, it occurred to me that Raymond would make a very fine runner. Doesn't he always keep up with me on my trots? And he surely knows how to breathe in counts of seven cause he's always doing it at the dinner table, which drives my brother George up the wall. And I'm smiling to beat the band cause if I've lost this race, or if me and Gretchen tied, or even if I've won, I can always retire as a runner and begin a whole new career as a coach with Raymond as my champion. After all, with a little more study I can beat Cynthia and her phony self at the spelling bee. And if I bugged my mother, I could get piano lessons and become a star. And I have a big rep as the baddest thing around. And I've got a roomful of ribbons and medals and awards. But what has Raymond got to call his own?

So I stand there with my new plans, laughing out loud by this time as Raymond jumps down from the fence and runs over with his teeth showing and his arms down to the side, which no one before him has quite mastered as a running style.

46

And by the time he comes over I'm jumping up and down so glad to see him—my brother Raymond, a great runner in the family tradition. But of course everyone thinks I'm jumping up and down because the men on the loudspeaker have finally gotten themselves together and compared notes and are announcing "In first place—Miss Hazel Elizabeth Deborah Parker." (Dig that.) "In second place—Miss Gretchen P. Lewis." And I look over at Gretchen wondering what the "P" stands for. And I smile. Cause she's good, no doubt about it. Maybe she'd like to help me coach Raymond; she obviously is serious about running, as any fool can see. And she nods to congratulate me and then she smiles. And I smile. We stand there with this big smile of respect between us. It's about as real a smile as girls can do for each other, considering we don't practice real smiling every day, you know, cause maybe we too busy being flowers or fairies or strawberries instead of something honest and worthy of respect . . . you know . . . like being people.

THE WITCH WHO CAME FOR THE WEEKEND

William Trevor

M iss Perego was wearing a black-and-white striped dress and a wide-brimmed white hat and dark glasses. She waved and smiled at Frances's father. Her teeth were white and there seemed to be a lot of them. She was carrying a small white suitcase and was accompanied by a man called Gareth.

"So this is Frances!" Miss Perego said. She smiled her large white smile and touched Frances's left cheek with the back of her left hand. Her flesh was cold. "So lovely to meet you, little Frances," Miss Perego murmured, and the man called Gareth smiled at Frances also.

Frances's father drove the car through the town and out into the country, through the village that was the nearest village to where Frances and her parents lived, and then through the lanes to the farmhouse. All the time Miss Perego talked. She talked about the theater because Miss Perego was an actress, although not a famous one. Frances had seen her once in a television advertisement for pipe tobacco, in which she looked just like a doll. She had to pretend to be a woman at a garden party who fell in love with a man because he smoked tobacco. Frances's parents had been excited by this, but Frances had considered the whole thing rather silly. In the car on the way to the farmhouse she realized that the man called Gareth was the man in the advertisement.

"My dear, how are you?" Miss Perego cried when Frances's mother came out of the farmhouse with the two collie dogs. "My dear, how gorgeous!" she cried when the collies barked at her.

It was a pleasant June evening and there was a smell of cows in the yard, and a smell of roses in the kitchen because Frances's mother had picked some specially and put them in two jugs on the dresser. "My dear, what gorgeous roses!" Miss Perego said, and Frances knew that when they all sat down to supper Miss Perego would say: "My dear, what gorgeous ham!" which ten minutes later Miss Perego did. The man called Gareth said the ham was gorgeous also.

Frances went to the primary school in the village that was nearest the farmhouse. Every morning she walked half a mile to the crossroads called Moor House Cross, where the school bus picked her up at half past eight, and every afternoon she walked home from the crossroads. Mr. Addleripe, who had been in every country in the world, drove the school bus and knew all about witches. After her mother and her father and her friend, Poppy Jones, Mr. Addleripe was the nicest person Frances knew. For the last mile of the journey home with him every afternoon, they were alone together in the bus, and often when he drew the bus up at Moor House Cross they sat awhile longer, chatting.

"I knew a witch in China," Mr. Addleripe said. "Extraordinary girl, no more than sixteen she was."

The witch in China could control flies, Mr. Addleripe said. A Chinese room would be full of flies and the sixteen-year-old witch would enter it and tell them to leave by the window and the flies immediately would. There was another witch he'd come across, a Mrs. Llewellyn who owned a chip shop in Swansea, who could control birds. Mrs. Llewellyn could stand in a field, still as a statue, and three minutes later birds would be perched all over her. She could walk about the field and the birds would remain with her, some of them apparently asleep.

Mr. Addleripe had known Australian and American witches as well as Welsh and Chinese witches. He'd known African witches who could kill you stone dead just by looking at you, and Egyptian and Norwegian witches and Sicilian witches. He'd known witches in Spain, Denmark, Hungary, and France. Twenty-five years ago he'd known one in Greece. Actually, Mr. Addleripe said, he'd made a study of witches.

A lot of nonsense was talked about witches, Mr. Addleripe said. For a start, no witch ever flew about on a broomstick, nor did witches insist on living in the heart of a forest with only a black cat for company. And all films, stories, and television programs that claimed witches could be here one moment and gone the next were rubbish. There was no such thing as a disappearing witch. If you came across a woman who could disappear like that you were probably in the company of a ghost.

When first he'd talked to her about witches, Frances began to look for them.

"Oh no, no," he said when she told him that. "You'll never come across a witch easily, Frances. Your real witch doesn't go around showing off her powers, you know. Your real witch keeps quiet as a mouse about her powers. Naturally enough, Frances: time was, when you caught your witch you burned her."

Nowadays, Mr. Addleripe explained, a lot of witches didn't want to be witches. A woman, for instance, might be able to make lemons roll upward on a slope, but she'd keep it to herself, because men were frightened of stuff like that and wouldn't want to marry such a creature. A woman might be able to control ants or bees or hold conversations with horses, but the current fashion was not to admit it. He'd known a woman who used to walk about in a cageful of tigers and another who could bring dead trees to life by touching them. They'd both been in love, the first with a circus clown and the second with a manager of an insurance company, but neither the clown nor the manager had wanted to marry them after they'd heard about the tigers and the trees.

You knew if a woman had witch's powers, Mr. Addleripe said, by the nervous way she stood and the nervous way she moved, and by the feel of her flesh. He explained in detail what he meant by the nervous way a witch stood and walked, and in the end Frances understood him. She used to get out of the bus at Moor House Cross and walk through the lanes to the farm-house, remembering what he'd said and thinking about it. She felt very curious about Mrs. Llewellyn who would stand in a field and three minutes later would be covered with birds, and about any woman who could hold conversations with horses, or control flies. She hoped she'd develop a witch's powers herself, but Mr. Addleripe said she definitely wouldn't. He could tell just by looking at her, he said.

"Really gorgeous!" Miss Perego said when she'd finished her ham and salad. "Oh, isn't it nice to be in the country!"

Frances considered that Miss Perego was probably the silliest person she'd ever listened to. Miss Perego had a way of flapping her long, thin hands in the air, and all during supper she kept her white hat on, and her sunglasses. She wasn't at all like

Frances's mother, who was pink cheeked and bustling, or like Frances's father, who didn't say much unless he had a joke to tell. The man called Gareth kept agreeing with everything Miss Perego said in a way that was silly also.

"My dear," Miss Perego said, "how gorgeous!"

"Gorgeous!" the man called Gareth said.

They were referring to a dish of strawberries that Frances's mother had placed on the table, and to the jug of yellow cream that went with them. How tedious the weekend was going to be, Frances thought, with Miss Perego saying everything was gorgeous all the time and the man called Gareth agreeing! She wondered where on earth her parents had come across Miss Perego, and seemed to remember her mother saying that they had known her for many years, long before she'd become an actress who wasn't quite famous.

Frances went to bed after the strawberries and cream. She lay awake for ten minutes, gloomily thinking about the boring weekend, with her mother occupied listening to Miss Perego's silly chatter and her father making hay, and the man called Gareth probably asleep somewhere. She knew that Mr. Addleripe would have said Miss Perego had a witch's powers because of the nervous way she'd stepped out of the train and because of her cold flesh. But if this was a witch, then a witch wasn't much to write home about. Mr. Addleripe might have said that Miss Perego was probably keeping her witch's powers to herself because she wanted the man called Gareth to marry her. What on earth good was a witch who kept her powers to herself?

Frances, having met, at last, a woman she could tell Mr. Addleripe about, felt most disappointed. She began to think that maybe Mr. Addleripe had been putting her on, that witches weren't a quarter as interesting as he'd made them out to be. "Really!" Frances contemptuously exclaimed before she went to sleep. "Really!"

The next morning Miss Perego sat at the kitchen table while Frances's mother made apple crumble, scones, two sponge cakes, and a fruitcake. Frances sat in a corner of the kitchen watching Miss Perego and listening to Miss Perego's silly conversation. The more she watched and listened the more she was convinced that Miss Perego had a witch's powers. She had all the nervousness that Mr. Addleripe had described, a nervousness that for all Frances knew could be the cause of her cold flesh.

"Why don't you go out and play, Frances?" Frances's mother said, beating up eggs.

Frances shook her head. Miss Perego laughed.

"Well, you can't sit there all morning, staring at poor Miss Perego. Why don't you go and watch them baling the hay?"

Frances shook her head again.

"Gareth's gone for a walk," Miss Perego said. "Why don't you go and look for him?"

"It's rude to stare, dear," Frances's mother said.

Miss Perego wasn't wearing her white hat, but she'd arrived down to breakfast with her sunglasses on and hadn't taken them off. She'd been sitting at the table for hours, talking about the theater. Usually on Saturday mornings Frances sat at the table herself, watching her mother and sometimes helping to mix the butter and sugar. She'd often told her mother what Mr. Addleripe said in the bus, about witches and the countries he'd visited and the habits that foreign people had, and about when he'd been a child.

"Why don't you ask Poppy over to play this afternoon?" her mother said.

Frances shook her head. She didn't want to ask Poppy Jones over, she said, because she and Poppy Jones weren't on speaking terms just at the moment.

Miss Perego laughed. "Let's go and look for Gareth," she said, and since her mother was glaring at her, Frances decided she'd better go.

They walked through the yard and across the paddock where Frances's father was rearing five heifers.

"We sometimes have lambs here," Frances told Miss Perego, knowing she had to be polite to the woman.

"How gorgeous!" Miss Perego said.

Frances led the way into the woods, presuming that the man called Gareth had gone there since it was the walk that people who came for the weekend usually went on. You skirted the big meadow and then clambered down the valley to the river. Miss Perego, Frances saw, would have difficulty because she was wearing unsuitable shoes. Typical, Frances thought.

"There's a man who drives the school bus," Frances said, "who knew a Chinese girl who could control flies."

"Eh?"

"If there were flies in a room this girl could make them go out of the window. Another woman, a Mrs. Llewellyn, could control birds. Mrs. Llewellyn keeps a chip shop in Swansea."

"Good heavens!"

"They're women with a witch's powers. Another woman Mr. Addleripe knew had conversations with horses."

Miss Perego, removing a length of bramble from her skirt, did not say anything.

"Another woman could bring dead trees to life by touching them."

"And can you do anything like that, Frances?"

55

"No. Can you, Miss Perego?"

Miss Perego laughed.

"It's all nonsense," Frances said, "witches having broomsticks and living in a forest. Witches are just like you and me, Miss Perego. Mr. Addleripe's made a study of them. Mr. Addleripe," Frances said, following Miss Perego over a stile, "taught me how to spot a witch at a glance."

"Good Lord!"

"It's easy, actually."

Again Miss Perego did not say anything. Frances walked beside her.

"You can tell by the way they move," Frances said, "and by the way they stand. And by the coldness of their flesh."

"I see," said Miss Perego.

"They're very nervous women, actually."

They crossed the river on stepping stones and climbed up through the trees on the other side. They emerged into a sunny field.

"Let's sit down," Miss Perego said.

They sat on the grass, among daisies and buttercups.

"What a funny man Mr. Addleripe sounds!" Miss Perego said.

"He's one of my best friends."

"Look," Miss Perego said.

She pointed at a grass snake that was wriggling its way toward Frances's right leg. Frances gasped. She didn't like snakes. She began to get to her feet but Miss Perego told her not to.

"Sit there," Miss Perego said in a sharp voice. "Sit there, Frances, and close your eyes."

The last thing Frances wanted to do was to close her eyes. If she closed her eyes she'd feel the grass snake crawling on her leg, and she shuddered even at the thought of it.

"Close your eyes," Miss Perego said again. All the silliness had gone out of her voice. "Close them."

Frances did so, and a second could hardly have passed before she heard Miss Perego telling her to open them again. "Quickly now," Miss Perego said in the same no-nonsense voice.

The grass snake was no longer there. It couldn't have crawled away in the time. There hadn't even been time for Miss Perego to have picked it up and thrown it into the trees.

"Where is it, Miss Perego?"

"Gone."

Frances began to get up again, but again Miss Perego told her not to.

"Look," Miss Perego said.

A ladybug was crawling onto Frances's right leg.

"I quite like ladybugs," Miss Perego said. "Don't you, Frances?"

"Yes."

"I'm so glad," Miss Perego said softly.

When Miss Perego said that, Francis began to feel frightened of her. She wished she hadn't stared at her in the kitchen. She wished she hadn't begun to talk about witches. It was one thing talking about witches in Mr. Addleripe's bus; it was quite another to be sitting in a field with a witch who'd just turned a grass snake into a ladybug. Miss Perego seemed all the more frightening because she'd been so silly and now was so serious. Miss Perego wasn't laughing, she wasn't even smiling. Not in a hundred years would you have guessed that Miss Perego had once been like a doll in a television advertisement for tobacco.

"Sounds a bit of a silly," Miss Perego said as softly as before, "that Mr. Addleripe."

"Oh, no . . ."

"Silly to talk about witches like that, I'd have said. Silly to be too interested, you know."

The ladybug crawled along Frances's leg. Did it know it was a ladybug? Frances wondered. Did it still imagine it was a grass snake? Would she know she was Frances if she changed into something else? Would she feel like Frances even though she'd suddenly become a horsefly?

"Ladybugs are harmless," Miss Perego said quietly.

They walked from the field together, down into the valley and across the stepping stones in the river and up the other side, skirting the meadow, through the paddock and the yard. At lunch Miss Perego was her old silly self again, and as Frances listened to her chatter and her laughter, she seemed more frightening even than she'd seemed before.

For the rest of that weekend Miss Perego giggled and said things were gorgeous. She said it was gorgeous that Frances's father had finished haymaking, and that the sponge cakes and the scones and the fruitcake were gorgeous. She sat at the kitchen table, chattering to Frances's mother. She said what fun it had been making the television advertisement for pipe tobacco.

"Good-bye, Frances," Miss Perego said on Sunday evening. She held out her right hand and Frances felt the cold flesh, and for a moment could hardly believe that any person could be so silly and also be so frightening. Miss Perego smiled at her.

"I hope the weekend wasn't too boring for you, Frances," Miss Perego said.

"Oh no, Miss Perego."

"Do give my love to that Mr. Addleripe of yours."

The next afternoon, when she sat alone with Mr. Addleripe in his bus, Frances wanted to tell him about Miss Perego and to ask him what he thought. She wanted to describe Miss Perego, her crowded mouthful of teeth and her dark glasses and her pretend silliness and her white hat. She wanted to mention the man called Gareth whom Miss Perego hoped to marry, who'd appeared in the tobacco advertisement with her. But she didn't.

"A nice lady came for the weekend," she said instead.

AS THE NIGHT THE DAY

Abioseh Nicol

Kojo and Bandele walked slowly across the hot green lawn, holding their science manuals with moist fingers. In the distance they could hear the junior school collecting in the hall of the main school building, for singing practice. Nearer, but still far enough, their classmates were strolling towards them. The two reached the science block and entered it. It was a low building set apart from the rest of the high school which sprawled on the hillside of the African savanna. The laboratory was a longish room and at one end they saw Basu, another boy, looking out of the window, his back turned to them. Mr. Abu, the ferocious laboratory attendant, was not about. The rows of multicoloured bottles looked inviting. A Bunsen burner soughed loudly in the heavy, weary heat. Where the tip of the light-blue triangle of flame ended, a shimmering plastic transparency started. One could see the restless hot air moving in the minute tornado. The two African boys watched it, interestedly, holding hands.

"They say it is hotter inside the flame than on its surface," Kojo said, doubtfully. "I wonder how they know."

"I think you mean the opposite; let's try it ourselves," Bandele answered.

"How?"

"Let's take the temperature inside."

"All right, here is a thermometer. You do it."

"It says ninety degrees now. I shall take the temperature of the outer flame first, then you can take the inner yellow one."

Bandele held the thermometer gently forward to the flame and Kojo craned to see. The thin thread of quicksilver shot upward within the stem of the instrument with swift malevolence and there was a slight crack. The stem had broken. On the bench the small bulbous drops of mercury which had spilled from it shivered with glinting, playful malice and shuddered down to the cement floor, dashing themselves into a thousand shining pieces, some of which coalesced again and shook gaily as if with silent laughter.

"Oh my God!" whispered Kojo hoarsely.

"Shut up!" Bandele said, imperiously, in a low voice.

Bandele swept the few drops on the bench into his cupped hand and threw the blob of mercury down the sink. He swept those on the floor under an adjoining cupboard with his bare feet. Then, picking up the broken halves of the thermometer, he tiptoed to the waste bin and dropped them in. He tiptoed back to Kojo, who was standing petrified by the blackboard.

"See no evil, hear no evil, speak no evil," he whispered to Kojo.

It all took place in a few seconds. Then the rest of the class started pouring in, chattering and pushing each other. Basu, who had been at the end of the room with his back turned to them all the time, now turned round and limped laboriously across to join the class, his eyes screwed up as they always were.

The class ranged itself loosely in a semicircle around the demonstration platform. They were dressed in the school uniform of white shirt and khaki shorts. Their official age was around sixteen although, in fact, it ranged from Kojo's fifteen years to one or two boys of twenty-one.

Mr. Abu, the laboratory attendant, came in from the adjoining store and briskly cleaned the blackboard. He was a retired African sergeant from the Army Medical Corps and was feared by the boys. If he caught any of them in any petty thieving, he offered them the choice of a hard smack on the bottom or of being reported to the science masters. Most boys chose the former as they knew the matter would end there with no protracted interviews, moral recrimination, and an entry in the conduct book.

The science master stepped in and stood on his small platform. A tall, thin, dignified Negro, with greying hair and silver-rimmed spectacles badly fitting on his broad nose and always slipping down, making him look avuncular. "Vernier" was his nickname as he insisted on exact measurement and exact speech "as fine as a vernier scale," he would say, which measured, of course, things in thousandths of a millimetre. Vernier set the experiments for the day and demonstrated them, then retired behind the *Church Times* which he read seriously in between walking quickly down the aisles of lab benches, advising boys. It was a simple heat experiment to show that a dark surface gave out more heat by radiation than a bright surface.

During the class, Vernier was called away to the telephone and Abu was not about, having retired to the lavatory for a smoke. As soon as a posted sentinel announced that he was out of sight, minor pandemonium broke out. Some of the boys raided the store. The wealthier ones swiped rubber tubing to make catapults and to repair bicycles, and helped themselves to chemicals for developing photographic films. The poorer boys were in deadlier earnest and took only things of strict commercial interest which could be sold easily in the market. They emptied stuff into bottles in their pockets. Soda for making soap, magnesium sulphate for opening medicine, salt for cooking, liquid paraffin for women's hairdressing, and fine yellow iodoform powder much in demand for sprinkling on sores. Kojo protested mildly against all this. "Oh, shut up!" a few boys said. Sorie, a huge boy who always wore a fez indoors and who, rumour said, had already fathered a child, commanded respect and some leadership in the class. He was sipping his favourite mixture of diluted alcohol and bicarbonate—which he called "gin and fizz"—from a beaker. "Look here, Kojo, you are getting out of hand. What do you think our parents pay taxes and school fees for? For us to enjoy—or to buy a new car every year for Simpson?" The other boys laughed. Simpson was the European headmaster, feared by the small boys, adored by the boys in the middle school, and liked, in a critical fashion, with reservations, by some of the senior boys and African masters. He had a passion for new motorcars, buying one yearly.

"Come to think of it," Sorie continued to Kojo, "you must take something yourself, then we'll know we are safe." "Yes, you must," the other boys insisted. Kojo gave in and, unwillingly, took a little nitrate for some gunpowder experiments which he was carrying out at home.

"Someone!" the lookout called.

The boys dispersed in a moment. Sorie swilled out his mouth at the sink with some water. Mr. Abu, the lab attendant, entered and observed the innocent collective expression of the class. He glared round suspiciously and sniffed the air. It was a physics experiment, but the place smelled chemical. However, Vernier came in then. After asking if anyone was in difficulties, and finding that no one could momentarily think up anything, he retired to his chair and settled down to an article on Christian reunion, adjusting his spectacles and thoughtfully sucking an empty tooth socket.

Towards the end of the period, the class collected around Vernier and gave in their results, which were then discussed. One of the more political boys asked Vernier: If dark surfaces gave out more heat, was that why they all had black faces in West Africa? A few boys giggled. Basu looked down and tapped his clubfoot embarrassedly on the floor. Vernier was used to questions of this sort from the senior boys. He never committed himself as he was getting near retirement and his pension, and became more guarded each year. He sometimes even feared that Simpson had spies among the boys.

"That may be so, although the opposite might be more convenient."

Everything in science had a loophole, the boys thought, and said so to Vernier.

"Ah! That is what is called research," he replied, enigmatically.

Sorie asked a question. Last time, they had been shown that an electric spark with hydrogen and oxygen atoms formed water. Why was not that method used to provide water in town at the height of the dry season when there was an acute water shortage?

"It would be too expensive," Vernier replied, shortly. He disliked Sorie, not because of his different religion, but because he thought that Sorie was a bad influence and also asked ridiculous questions.

Sorie persisted. There was plenty of water during the rainy season. It could be split by lightning to hydrogen and oxygen in October and the gases compressed and stored, then changed back to water in March during the shortage. There was a faint ripple of applause from Sorie's admirers.

"It is an impracticable idea," Vernier snapped.

The class dispersed and started walking back across the hot grass. Kojo and Bandele heaved sighs of relief and joined Sorie's crowd, which was always the largest.

"Science is a bit of a swindle," Sorie was saying. "I do not for a moment think that Vernier believes any of it himself," he continued. "Because, if he does, why is he always reading religious books?"

"Come back, all of you, come back!" Mr. Abu's stentorian voice rang out, across to them.

They wavered and stopped. Kojo kept walking on in a blind panic.

"Stop," Bandele hissed across. "You fool." He stopped, turned, and joined the returning crowd, closely followed by Bandele. Abu joined Vernier on the platform. The loose semi-circle of boys faced them.

"Mr. Abu just found this in the waste bin," Vernier announced, grey with anger. He held up the two broken halves of the thermometer. "It must be due to someone from this class as the number of thermometers was checked before being put out."

A little wind gusted in through the window and blew the silence heavily this way and that.

"Who?"

No one answered. Vernier looked round and waited.

"Since no one has owned up, I am afraid I shall have to detain you for an hour after school as punishment," said Vernier.

There was a murmur of dismay and anger. An important soccer house match was scheduled for that afternoon. Some boys put their hands up and said that they had to play in the match.

"I don't care," Vernier shouted. He felt, in any case, that too much time was devoted to games and not enough to work.

He left Mr. Abu in charge and went off to fetch his things from the main building.

"We shall play 'Bible and Key,'" Abu announced as soon as Vernier had left. Kojo had been afraid of this and new beads of perspiration sprang from his troubled brow. All the boys knew the details. It was a method of finding out a culprit by divination. A large door key was placed between the leaves of a Bible at the New Testament passage where Ananias and Sapphira were struck dead before the Apostles for lying, and the Bible suspended by two bits of string tied to both ends of the key. The combination was held up by someone and the names of all present were called out in turn. When that of the sinner was called, the Bible was expected to turn round and round violently and fall.

Now Abu asked for a Bible. Someone produced a copy. He opened the first page and then shook his head and handed it back. "This won't do," he said, "it's a Revised Version; only the genuine Word of God will give us the answer."

An Authorized King James Version was then produced and he was satisfied. Soon he had the contraption fixed up. He looked round the semicircle from Sorie at one end, through the others, to Bandele, Basu, and Kojo at the other, near the door.

"You seem to have an honest face," he said to Kojo. "Come and hold it." Kojo took the ends of the string gingerly with both hands, trembling slightly.

Abu moved over to the low window and stood at attention, his sharp profile outlined against the red hibiscus flowers, the green trees, and the molten sky. The boys watched anxiously. A black-bodied lizard scurried up a wall and started nodding its pink head with grave impartiality.

Abu fixed his aging bloodshot eyes on the suspended Bible.
He spoke hoarsely and slowly:

Oh, Bible, Bible, on a key,
Kindly tell it unto me,
By swinging slowly round and true,
To whom this sinful act is due. . . .

He turned to the boys and barked out their names in a
parade-ground voice, beginning with Sorie and working his
way round, looking at the Bible after each name.

To Kojo, trembling and shivering as if ice-cold water had
been thrown over him, it seemed as if he had lost all power and
that some gigantic being stood behind him holding up his tired
aching elbows. It seemed to him as if the key and Bible had
taken on a life of their own, and he watched with fascination
the whole combination moving slowly, jerkily, and rhythmi-
cally in short arcs as if it had acquired a heartbeat.

"Ayo Sogbenri, Sonnir Kargbo, Oji Ndebu." Abu was
coming to the end now. "Tommy Longe, Ajayi Cole, Bandele
Fagb . . ."

Kojo dropped the Bible. "I am tired," he said, in a small
scream. "I am tired."

"Yes, he is," Abu agreed, "but we are almost finished; only
Bandele and Basu are left."

"Pick up that book, Kojo, and hold it up again." Bandele's
voice whipped through the air with cold fury. It sobered Kojo
and he picked it up.

"Will you continue please with my name, Mr. Abu?" Bandele
asked, turning to the window.

"Go back to your place quickly, Kojo," Abu said. "Vernier is
coming. He might be vexed. He is a strongly religious man and
so does not believe in the 'Bible and Key' ceremony."

Kojo slipped back with sick relief, just before Vernier entered.

In the distance the rest of the school were assembling for closing prayers. The class sat and stood around the blackboard and demonstration bench in attitudes of exasperation, resignation, and self-righteous indignation. Kojo's heart was beating so loudly that he was surprised no one else heard it.

Once to every man and nation
Comes the moment to decide . . .

The closing hymn floated across to them, interrupting the still afternoon.

Kojo got up. He felt now that he must speak the truth, or life would be intolerable ever afterwards. Bandele got up swiftly before him. In fact, several things seemed to happen all at the same time. The rest of the class stirred. Vernier looked up from a book review which he had started reading. A butterfly, with black and gold wings, flew in and sat on the edge of the blackboard, flapping its wings quietly and waiting too.

"Basu was here first before any of the class," Bandele said firmly.

Everyone turned to Basu, who cleared his throat.

"I was just going to say so myself, sir," Basu replied to Vernier's inquiring glance.

"Pity you had no thought of it before," Vernier said, dryly. "What were you doing here?"

"I missed the previous class, so I came straight to the lab and waited. I was over there by the window, trying to look at the blue sky. I did not break the thermometer, sir."

A few boys tittered. Some looked away. The others muttered. Basu's breath always smelt of onions, but although he could play no games, some boys liked him and were kind to him in a tolerant way.

"Well if you did not, someone did. We shall continue with the detention."

Vernier noticed Abu standing by. "You need not stay, Mr. Abu," he said to him. "I shall close up. In fact, come with me now and I shall let you out through the back gate."

He went out with Abu.

When he had left, Sorie turned to Basu and asked mildly: "You are sure you did not break it?"

"No, I didn't."

"He did it," someone shouted.

"But what about the 'Bible and Key'?" Basu protested. "It did not finish. Look at him." He pointed to Bandele.

"I was quite willing for it to go on," said Bandele. "You were the only one left."

Someone threw a book at Basu and said, "Confess!"

Basu backed onto a wall. "To God, I shall call the police if anyone strikes me," he cried fiercely.

"He thinks he can buy the police," a voice called.

"That proves it," someone shouted from the back.

"Yes, he must have done it," the others said, and they started throwing books at Basu. Sorie waved his arm for them to stop, but they did not. Books, corks, boxes of matches rained on Basu. He bent his head and shielded his face with his bent arm.

"I did not do it, I swear I did not do it. Stop it, you fellows," he moaned over and over again. A small cut had appeared on his temple and he was bleeding. Kojo sat quietly for a while. Then a curious hum started to pass through him, and his hands began to tremble, his armpits to feel curiously wetter. He turned round and picked up a book and flung it with desperate force at Basu, and then another. He felt somehow that there was an awful swelling of guilt which he could only shed by

70

punishing himself through hurting someone. Anger and rage against everything different seized him, because if everything and everyone had been the same, somehow he felt nothing would have been wrong and they would all have been happy. He was carried away now by a torrent which swirled and pounded. He felt that somehow Basu was in the wrong, must be in the wrong, and if he hurt him hard enough he would convince the others and therefore himself that he had not broken the thermometer and that he had never done anything wrong. He groped for something bulky enough to throw, and picked up the Bible.

"Stop it," Vernier shouted through the open doorway. "Stop it, you hooligans, you beasts."

They all became quiet and shamefacedly put down what they were going to throw. Basu was crying quietly and hopelessly, his thin body shaking.

"Go home, all of you, go home. I am ashamed of you." His black face shone with anger. "You are an utter disgrace to your nation and to your race."

They crept away, quietly, uneasily, avoiding each other's eyes, like people caught in a secret passion.

Vernier went to the first-aid cupboard and started dressing Basu's wounds.

Kojo and Bandele came back and hid behind the door, listening. Bandele insisted that they should.

Vernier put Basu's bandaged head against his waistcoat and dried the boy's tears with his handkerchief, gently patting his shaking shoulders.

"It wouldn't have been so bad if I had done it, sir," he mumbled, snuggling his head against Vernier, "but I did not do it. I swear to God I did not."

"Hush, hush," said Vernier comfortingly.

"Now they will hate me even more," he moaned.

"Hush, hush."

"I don't mind the wounds so much, they will heal."

"Hush, hush."

"They've missed the football match and now they will never talk to me again, oh-ee, oh-ee, why have I been so punished?"

"As you grow older," Vernier advised, "you must learn that men are punished not always for what they do, but often for what people think they will do, or for what they are. Remember that and you will find it easier to forgive them. 'To thine own self be true!'" Vernier ended with a flourish, holding up his clenched fist in a mock dramatic gesture, quoting from the Shakespeare examination set book for the year and declaiming to the dripping taps and empty benches and still afternoon, to make Basu laugh.

Basu dried his eyes and smiled wanly and replied: "'And it shall follow as the night the day.' *Hamlet*, act one, scene three, Polonius to Laertes."

"There's a good chap. First Class, Grade One. I shall give you a lift home."

Kojo and Bandele walked down the red laterite road together, Kojo dispiritedly kicking stones into the gutter.

"The fuss they made over a silly old thermometer," Bandele began.

"I don't know, old man, I don't know," Kojo said impatiently.

They had both been shaken by the scene in the empty lab. A thin invisible wall of hostility and mistrust was slowly rising between them.

"Basu did not do it, of course," Bandele said.

Kojo stopped dead in his tracks. "Of course he did not do it," he shouted; "we did it."

"No need to shout, old man. After all, it was your idea."

"It wasn't," Kojo said furiously. "You suggested we try it."

"Well, you started the argument. Don't be childish." They tramped on silently, raising small clouds of dust with their bare feet.

"I should not take it too much to heart," Bandele continued. "That chap Basu's father hoards foodstuff like rice and palm oil until there is a shortage and then sells them at high prices. The police are watching him."

"What has that got to do with it?" Kojo asked.

"Don't you see, Basu might quite easily have broken that thermometer. I bet he has done things before that we have all been punished for." Bandele was emphatic.

They walked on steadily down the main road of the town, past the Syrian and Lebanese shops crammed with knick-knacks and rolls of cloth, past a large Indian shop with dull red carpets and brass trays displayed in its windows, carefully step-ping aside in the narrow road as the British officials sped by in cars to their hill-station bungalows for lunch and siesta.

Kojo reached home at last. He washed his feet and ate his main meal for the day. He sat about heavily and restlessly for some hours. Night soon fell with its usual swiftness, at six, and he finished his homework early and went to bed.

Lying in bed he rehearsed again what he was determined to do the next day. He would go up to Vernier:

"Sir," he would begin, "I wish to speak with you privately."

"Can it wait?" Vernier would ask.

"No, sir," he would say firmly, "as a matter of fact it is rather urgent."

Vernier would take him to an empty classroom and say, "What is troubling you, Kojo Ananse?"

"I wish to make a confession, sir. I broke the thermometer yesterday." He had decided he would not name Bandele; it was up to the latter to decide whether he would lead a pure life.

Vernier would adjust his slipping glasses up his nose and think. Then he would say:

"This is a serious matter, Kojo. You realize you should have confessed yesterday?"

"Yes, sir, I am very sorry."

"You have done great harm, but better late than never. You will, of course, apologize in front of the class and particularly to Basu who has shown himself a finer chap than all of you."

"I shall do so, sir."

"Why have you come to me now to apologize? Were you hoping that I would simply forgive you?"

"I was hoping you would, sir. I was hoping you would show your forgiveness by beating me."

Vernier would pull his glasses up his nose again. He would move his tongue inside his mouth reflectively. "I think you are right. Do you feel you deserve six strokes or nine?"

"Nine, sir."

"Bend over!"

Kojo had decided he would not cry because he was almost a man.

Whack! Whack!!

Lying in bed in the dark thinking about it all as it would happen tomorrow, he clenched his teeth and tensed his buttocks in imaginary pain.

Whack! Whack!! Whack!!!

Suddenly, in his little room, under his thin cotton sheet, he began to cry. Because he felt the sharp lancing pain already cutting into him. Because of Basu and Simpson and the thermometer. For all the things he wanted to do and be which would never happen. For all the good men they had told them about, Jesus Christ, Mohammed, and George Washington who never told a lie. For Florence Nightingale and David Livingstone. For Kagawa, the Japanese man, for Gandhi, and for Kwegyir Aggrey, the African. Oh-ee, oh-ee. Because he knew he would never be as straight and strong and true as the school song said they should be. He saw, for the first time, what this thing would be like, becoming a man. He touched the edge of an inconsolable eternal grief. Oh-ee, oh-ee; always, he felt, always I shall be a disgrace to the nation and the race.

His mother passed by his bedroom door, slowly dragging her slippered feet as she always did. He pushed his face into his wet pillow to stifle his sobs, but she had heard him. She came in and switched on the light.

"What is the matter with you, my son?"

He pushed his face farther into his pillow.

"Nothing," he said, muffled and choking.

"You have been looking like a sick fowl all afternoon," she continued.

She advanced and put the back of her moist cool fingers against the side of his neck.

"You have got fever," she exclaimed. "I'll get something from the kitchen."

When she had gone out, Kojo dried his tears and turned the dry side of the pillow up. His mother reappeared with a thermometer in one hand and some quinine mixture in the other.

"Oh, take it away, take it away," he shouted, pointing to her right hand and shutting his eyes tightly.

"All right, all right," she said, slipping the thermometer into her bosom.

He is a queer boy, she thought, with pride and a little fear as she watched him drink the clear bitter fluid.

She then stood by him and held his head against her broad thigh as he sat up on the low bed, and she stroked his face. She knew he had been crying but did not ask him why, because she was sure he would not tell her. She knew he was learning, first slowly and now quickly, and she would soon cease to be his mother and be only one of the womenfolk in the family. Such a short time, she thought, when they are really yours and tell you everything. She sighed and slowly eased his sleeping head down gently.

The next day Kojo got to school early, and set to things briskly. He told Bandele that he was going to confess but would not name him. He half hoped he would join him. But Bandele had said, threateningly, that he had better not mention his name, let him go and be a Boy Scout on his own. The sneer strengthened him and he went off to the lab. He met Mr. Abu and asked for Vernier. Abu said Vernier was busy and what was the matter, anyhow.

"I broke the thermometer yesterday," Kojo said in a business-like manner.

Abu put down the glassware he was carrying.

"Well, I never!" he said. "What do you think you will gain by this?"

"I broke it," Kojo repeated.

"Basu broke it," Abu said impatiently. "Sorie got him to confess and Basu himself came here this morning and told the science master and myself that he knew now that he had knocked the thermometer by mistake when he came in early yesterday afternoon. He had not turned round to look, but he had definitely heard a tinkle as he walked by. Someone must have picked it up and put it in the waste bin. The whole matter is settled, the palaver finished."

He tapped a barometer on the wall and, squinting, read the pressure. He turned again to Kojo.

"I should normally have expected him to say so yesterday and save you boys missing the game. But there you are," he added, shrugging and trying to look reasonable, "you cannot hope for too much from a Syrian boy."

The Parsley Garden

William Saroyan

One day in August Al Condraj was wandering through Woolworth's without a penny to spend when he saw a small hammer that was not a toy but a real hammer, and he was possessed with a longing to have it. He believed it was just what he needed by which to break the monotony and with which to make something. He had gathered some first-class nails from Foley's Packing House where the boxmakers worked and where they had carelessly dropped at least fifteen cents' worth. He had gladly gone to the trouble of gathering them together because it had seemed to him that a nail, as such, was not something to be wasted. He had the nails, perhaps a half pound of them, at least two hundred of them, in a paper bag in the apple box in which he kept his junk at home.

Now, with the ten-cent hammer he believed he could make something out of box wood and the nails, although he had no idea what. Some sort of a table perhaps, or a small bench.

At any rate he took the hammer and slipped it into the pocket of his overalls, but just as he did so a man took him firmly by the arm without a word and pushed him to the back of the store into a small office. Another man, an older one, was seated behind a desk in the office, working with papers. The younger man, the one who had captured him, was excited and his forehead was covered with sweat.

"Well," he said, "here's one more of them."

The man behind the desk got to his feet and looked Al Condraj up and down.

"What's *he* swiped?"

"A hammer." The young man looked at Al with hatred. "Hand it over," he said.

The boy brought the hammer out of his pocket and handed it to the young man, who said, "I ought to hit you over the head with it, that's what I ought to do."

He turned to the older man, the boss, the manager of the store, and he said, "What do you want me to do with him?"

"Leave him with me," the older man said.

The younger man stepped out of the office, and the older man sat down and went back to work. Al Condraj stood in the office fifteen minutes before the older man looked at him again.

"Well," he said.

Al didn't know what to say. The man wasn't looking at him, he was looking at the door.

Finally Al said, "I didn't mean to steal it. I just need it and I haven't got any money."

"Just because you haven't got any money doesn't mean you've got a right to steal things," the man said. "Now, does it?"

"No, sir."

"Well, what am I going to do with you? Turn you over to the police?"

Al didn't say anything, but he certainly didn't want to be turned over to the police. He hated the man, but at the same time he realized somebody else could be a lot tougher than he was being.

"If I let you go, will you promise never to steal from this store again?"

"Yes, sir."

"All right," the man said. "Go out this way and don't come back to this store until you've got some money to spend."

He opened a door to the hall that led to the alley, and Al Condraj hurried down the hall and out into the alley.

The first thing he did when he was free was laugh, but he knew he had been humiliated, and he was deeply ashamed. It was not in his nature to take things that did not belong to him. He hated the young man who had caught him and he hated the manager of the store who had made him stand in silence in the office so long. He hadn't liked it at all when the young man had said he ought to hit him over the head with the hammer.

He should have had the courage to look him straight in the eye and say, "You and who else?"

Of course he *had* stolen the hammer and he had been caught, but it seemed to him he oughtn't to have been so humiliated.

After he had walked three blocks he decided he didn't want to go home just yet, so he turned around and started walking back to town. He almost believed he meant to go back and say something to the young man who had caught him. And then he wasn't sure he didn't mean to go back and steal the hammer again, and this time *not* get caught. As long as he had been made to feel like a thief anyway, the least he ought to get out of it was the hammer.

Outside the store he lost his nerve, though. He stood in the street, looking in, for at least ten minutes.

Then, crushed and confused and now bitterly ashamed of himself, first for having stolen something, then for having been caught, then for having been humiliated, then for not having guts enough to go back and do the job right, he began walking home again, his mind so troubled that he didn't greet his pal Pete Wawchek when they came face to face outside Graf's Hardware.

When he got home he was too ashamed to go inside and examine his junk, so he had a long drink of water from the faucet in the backyard. The faucet was used by his mother to water the stuff she planted every year: okra, bell peppers, tomatoes, cucumbers, onions, garlic, mint, eggplants, and parsley.

His mother called the whole business the parsley garden, and every night in the summer she would bring chairs out of the house and put them around the table she had had Ondro, the neighborhood handyman, make for her for fifteen cents, and she would sit at the table and enjoy the cool of the garden and the smell of the things she had planted and tended.

Sometimes she would even make a salad and moisten the flat old-country bread and slice some white cheese, and she and he would have supper in the parsley garden. After supper she would attach the water hose to the faucet and water her plants and the place would be cooler than ever and it would smell real good, real fresh and cool and green, all the different growing things making a green-garden smell out of themselves and the air and the water.

After the long drink of water he sat down where the parsley itself was growing and he pulled a handful of it out and slowly ate it. Then he went inside and told his mother what had happened. He even told her what he had *thought* of doing after he had been turned loose: to go back and steal the hammer again.

"I don't want you to steal," his mother said in broken English. "Here is ten cents. You go back to that man and you give him this money and you bring it home, that hammer."

"No," Al Condraj said. "I won't take your money for something I don't really need. I just thought I ought to have a hammer, so I could make something if I felt like it. I've got a lot of nails and some box wood, but I haven't got a hammer."

"Go buy it, that hammer," his mother said.

"No," Al said.

"All right," his mother said. "Shut up."

That's what she always said when she didn't know what else to say.

Al went out and sat on the steps. His humiliation was beginning to really hurt now. He decided to wander off along the railroad tracks to Foley's because he needed to think about it some more. At Foley's he watched Johnny Gale nailing boxes for ten minutes, but Johnny was too busy to notice him or talk to him, although one day at Sunday school, two or three years ago, Johnny had greeted him and said, "How's the boy?" Johnny worked with a boxmaker's hatchet and everybody in Fresno said he was the fastest boxmaker in town. He was the closest thing to a machine any packing house ever saw. Foley himself was proud of Johnny Gale.

Al Condraj finally set out for home because he didn't want to get in the way. He didn't want somebody working hard to notice that he was being watched and maybe say to him, "Go on, beat it." He didn't want Johnny Gale to do something like that. He didn't want to invite another humiliation.

On the way home he looked for money but all he found was the usual pieces of broken glass and rusty nails, the things that were always cutting his bare feet every summer.

When he got home his mother had made a salad and set the table, so he sat down to eat, but when he put the food in his mouth he just didn't care for it. He got up and went into the three-room house and got his apple box out of the corner of his room and went through his junk. It was all there, the same as yesterday.

He wandered off back to town and stood in front of the closed store, hating the young man who had caught him, and then he went along to the Hippodrome and looked at the display photographs from the two movies that were being shown that day.

Then he went along to the public library to have a look at all the books again, but he didn't like any of them, so he wandered around town some more, and then around half past eight he went home and went to bed.

His mother had already gone to bed because she had to be up at five to go to work at Inderrieden's, packing figs. Some days there would be work all day, some days there would be only half a day of it, but whatever his mother earned during the summer had to keep them the whole year.

He didn't sleep much that night because he couldn't get over what had happened, and he went over six or seven ways by which to adjust the matter. He went so far as to believe it would be necessary to kill the young man who had caught him. He also believed it would be necessary for him to steal systematically and successfully the rest of his life. It was a hot night and he couldn't sleep.

Finally, his mother got up and walked barefooted to the kitchen for a drink of water and on the way back she said to him softly, "Shut up."

When she got up at five in the morning he was out of the house, but that had happened many times before. He was a restless boy, and he kept moving all the time every summer. He was making mistakes and paying for them, and he had just tried stealing and had been caught at it and he was troubled. She fixed her breakfast, packed her lunch, and hurried off to work, hoping it would be a full day.

It was a full day, and then there was overtime, and although she had no more lunch she decided to work on for the extra money, anyway. Almost all the other packers were staying on, too, and her neighbor across the alley, Leeza Ahboot, who worked beside her, said, "Let us work until the work stops, then we'll go home and fix a supper between us and eat it in your parsley garden where it's so cool. It's a hot day and there's no sense not making an extra fifty or sixty cents."

When the two women reached the garden it was almost nine o'clock, but still daylight, and she saw her son nailing pieces of box wood together, making something with a hammer. It looked like a bench. He had already watered the garden and tidied up the rest of the yard, and the place seemed very nice, and her son seemed very serious and busy. She and Leeza went straight to work for their supper, picking bell peppers and tomatoes and cucumbers and a great deal of parsley for the salad.

Then Leeza went to her house for some bread which she had baked the night before, and some white cheese, and in a few minutes they were having supper together and talking pleasantly about the successful day they had had. After supper, they made Turkish coffee over an open fire in the yard. They drank the coffee and smoked a cigarette apiece, and told one another stories about their experiences in the old country and here in Fresno, and then they looked into their cups at the grounds to see if any good fortune was indicated, and there was: health and work and supper out of doors in the summer and enough money for the rest of the year.

Al Condraj worked and overheard some of the things they said, and then Leeza went home to go to bed, and his mother said, "Where you get it, that hammer, Al?"

"I got it at the store."

"How you get it? You steal it?"

Al Condraj finished the bench and sat on it. "No," he said. "I didn't steal it."

"How you get it?"

"I worked at the store for it," Al said.

"The store where you steal it yesterday?"

"Yes."

"Who give you job?"

"The boss."

"What you do?"

"I carried different stuff to the different counters."

"Well, that's good," the woman said. "How long you work for that little hammer?"

"I worked all day," Al said. "Mr. Clemmer gave me the hammer after I'd worked one hour, but I went right on working. The fellow who caught me yesterday showed me what to do, and we worked together. We didn't talk, but at the end of the day he took me to Mr. Clemmer's office and he told Mr. Clemmer that I'd worked hard all day and ought to be paid at least a dollar."

"That's good," the woman said.

"So Mr. Clemmer put a silver dollar on his desk for me, and then the fellow who caught me yesterday told him the store needed a boy like me every day, for a dollar a day, and Mr. Clemmer said I could have the job."

"That's good," the woman said. "You can make it a little money for yourself."

"I left the dollar on Mr. Clemmer's desk," Al Condraj said, "and I told them both I didn't want the job."

"Why you say that?" the woman said. "Dollar a day for eleven-year-old boy good money. Why you not take job?"

"Because I hate the both of them," the boy said. "I would never work for people like that. I just looked at them and picked up my hammer and walked out. I came home and I made this bench."

"All right," his mother said. "Shut up."

His mother went inside and went to bed, but Al Condraj sat on the bench he had made and smelled the parsley garden and didn't feel humiliated anymore.

But nothing could stop him from hating the two men, even though he knew they hadn't done anything they shouldn't have done.

THE VELDT

Ray Bradbury

"George, I wish you'd look at the nursery."

"What's wrong with it?"

"I don't know."

"Well, then."

"I just want you to look at it, is all, or call a psychologist in to look at it."

"What would a psychologist want with a nursery?"

"You know very well what he'd want." His wife paused in the middle of the kitchen and watched the stove busy humming to itself, making supper for four.

"It's just that the nursery is different now than it was."

"All right, let's have a look."

They walked down the hall of their soundproofed Happylife Home, which had cost them thirty thousand dollars installed, this house which clothed and fed and rocked them to sleep and played and sang and was good to them. Their approach sensitized a switch somewhere and the nursery light flicked on when they came within ten feet of it. Similarly, behind them, in the halls, lights went on and off as they left them behind, with a soft automaticity.

"Well," said George Hadley.

They stood on the thatched floor of the nursery. It was forty feet across by forty feet long and thirty feet high; it had cost half again as much as the rest of the house. "But nothing's too good for our children," George had said.

The nursery was silent. It was empty as a jungle glade at hot high noon. The walls were blank and two-dimensional. Now, as George and Lydia Hadley stood in the center of the room, the walls began to purr and recede into crystalline distance, it seemed, and presently an African veldt appeared, in three dimensions, on all sides, in color, reproduced to the final pebble and bit of straw. The ceiling above them became a deep sky with a hot yellow sun.

George Hadley felt the perspiration start on his brow.

"Let's get out of this sun," he said. "This is a little too real. But I don't see anything wrong."

"Wait a moment, you'll see," said his wife.

Now the hidden odorophonics were beginning to blow a wind of odor at the two people in the middle of the baked veldtland. The hot straw smell of lion grass, the cool green smell of the hidden water hole, the great rusty smell of animals, the smell of dust like a red paprika in the hot air. And now the sounds: the thump of distant antelope feet on grassy sod, the papery rustling of vultures. A shadow passed through the sky. The shadow flickered on George Hadley's upturned, sweating face.

"Filthy creatures," he heard his wife say.

"The vultures."

"You see, there are the lions, far over, that way. Now they're on their way to the water hole. They've just been eating," said Lydia. "I don't know what."

"Some animal." George Hadley put his hand up to shield off the burning light from his squinted eyes. "A zebra or a baby giraffe, maybe."

"Are you sure?" His wife sounded peculiarly tense.

"No, it's a little late to be *sure*," he said, amused. "Nothing over there I can see but cleaned bone, and the vultures dropping for what's left."

"Did you hear that scream?" she asked.

"No."

"About a minute ago?"

"Sorry, no."

The lions were coming. And again George Hadley was filled with admiration for the mechanical genius who had conceived this room. A miracle of efficiency selling for an absurdly low price. Every home should have one. Oh, occasionally they frightened you with their clinical accuracy, they startled you, gave you a twinge, but most of the time what fun for everyone, not only your own son and daughter, but for yourself when you felt like a quick jaunt to a foreign land, a quick change of scenery. Well, here it was!

And here were the lions now, fifteen feet away, so real, so feverishly and startlingly real that you could feel the prickling fur on your hand, and your mouth was stuffed with the dusty upholstery smell of their heated pelts, and the yellow of them was in your eyes like the yellow of an exquisite French tapestry, the yellows of lions and summer grass, and the sound of the matted lion lungs exhaling on the silent noontide, and the smell of meat from the panting, dripping mouths.

The lions stood looking at George and Lydia Hadley with terrible green-yellow eyes.

"Watch out!" screamed Lydia.

The lions came running at them.

Lydia bolted and ran. Instinctively, George sprang after her. Outside, in the hall, with the door slammed, he was laughing and she was crying, and they both stood appalled at the other's reaction.

"George!"

"Lydia! Oh, my dear poor sweet Lydia!"

"They almost got us!"

"Walls, Lydia, remember; crystal walls, that's all they are. Oh, they look real, I must admit—Africa in your parlor—but it's all dimensional, superreactionary, supersensitive color film and mental tape film behind glass screens. It's all odorophonics and sonics, Lydia. Here's my handkerchief."

"I'm afraid." She came to him and put her body against him and cried steadily. "Did you see? Did you *feel*? It's too real."

"Now, Lydia . . ."

"You've got to tell Wendy and Peter not to read any more on Africa."

"Of course—of course." He patted her.

"Promise?"

"Sure."

"And lock the nursery for a few days until I get my nerves settled."

"You know how difficult Peter is about that. When I punished him a month ago by locking the nursery for even a few hours—the tantrum he threw! And Wendy too. They *live* for the nursery."

"It's got to be locked, that's all there is to it."

"All right." Reluctantly he locked the huge door. "You've been working too hard. You need a rest."

"I don't know—I don't know," she said, blowing her nose, sitting down in a chair that immediately began to rock and comfort her. "Maybe I don't have enough to do. Maybe I have time to think too much. Why don't we shut the whole house off for a few days and take a vacation?"

"You mean you want to fry my eggs for me?"

"Yes." She nodded.

"And darn my socks?"

"Yes." A frantic, watery-eyed nodding.

"And sweep the house?"

"Yes, yes—oh, yes!"

"But I thought that's why we bought this house, so we wouldn't have to do anything?"

"That's just it. I feel like I don't belong here. The house is wife and mother now, and nursemaid. Can I compete with an African veldt? Can I give a bath and scrub the children as efficiently or quickly as the automatic scrub bath can? I cannot. And it isn't just me. It's you. You've been awfully nervous lately."

"I suppose I have been smoking too much."

"You look as if you don't know what to do with yourself in this house, either. You smoke a little more every morning and drink a little more every afternoon and need a little more sedative every night. You're beginning to feel unnecessary too."

"Am I?" He paused and tried to feel into himself to see what was really there.

"Oh, George!" She looked beyond him, at the nursery door. "Those lions can't get out of there, can they?"

He looked at the door and saw it tremble as if something had jumped against it from the other side.

"Of course not," he said.

At dinner they ate alone, for Wendy and Peter were at a special plastic carnival across town and had televised home to say they'd be late, to go ahead eating. So George Hadley, bemused, sat watching the dining room table produce warm dishes of food from its mechanical interior.

"We forgot the ketchup," he said.

"Sorry," said a small voice within the table, and ketchup appeared.

As for the nursery, thought George Hadley, it won't hurt for the children to be locked out of it awhile. Too much of anything isn't good for anyone. And it was clearly indicated that the children had been spending a little too much time on Africa. That *sun*. He could feel it on his neck, still, like a hot paw. And the *lions*. And the smell of blood. Remarkable how the nursery caught the telepathic emanations of the children's minds and created life to fill their every desire. The children thought lions, and there were lions. The children thought zebras, and there were zebras. Sun—sun. Giraffes—giraffes. Death and death.

That *last*. He chewed tastelessly on the meat that the table had cut for him. Death thoughts. They were awfully young, Wendy and Peter, for death thoughts. Or, no, you were never too young, really. Long before you knew what death was you were wishing it on someone else. When you were two years old you were shooting people with cap pistols.

But this—the long, hot African veldt—the awful death in the jaws of a lion. And repeated again and again.

"Where are you going?"

He didn't answer Lydia. Preoccupied, he let the lights glow softly on ahead of him, extinguish behind him as he padded to the nursery door. He listened against it. Far away, a lion roared.

He unlocked the door and opened it. Just before he stepped inside, he heard a faraway scream. And then another roar from the lions, which subsided quickly.

He stepped into Africa. How many times in the last year had he opened this door and found Wonderland, Alice, the

Mock Turtle, or Aladdin and his Magical Lamp, or Jack Pumpkinhead of Oz, or Dr. Dolittle, or the cow jumping over a very real-appearing moon—all the delightful contraptions of a make-believe world. How often had he seen Pegasus flying in the sky ceiling, or seen fountains of red fireworks, or heard angel voices singing. But now, this yellow hot Africa, this bake oven with murder in the heat. Perhaps Lydia was right. Perhaps they needed a little vacation from the fantasy which was growing a bit too real for ten-year-old children. It was all right to exercise one's mind with gymnastic fantasies, but when the lively child mind settled on *one* pattern . . . ? It seemed that, at a distance, for the past month, he had heard lions roaring, and smelled their strong odor seeping as far away as his study door. But, being busy, he had paid it no attention.

George Hadley stood on the African grassland alone. The lions looked up from their feeding, watching him. The only flaw to the illusion was the open door through which he could see his wife, far down the dark hall, like a framed picture, eating her dinner abstractedly.

"Go away," he said to the lions.

They did not go.

He knew the principle of the room exactly. You sent out your thoughts. Whatever you thought would appear.

"Let's have Aladdin and his lamp," he snapped.

The veldtland remained; the lions remained.

"Come on, room! I demand Aladdin!" he said.

Nothing happened. The lions mumbled in their baked pelts.

"Aladdin!"

He went back to dinner. "The fool room's out of order," he said. "It won't respond."

"Or—"

"Or what?"

"Or it *can't* respond," said Lydia, "because the children have thought about Africa and lions and killing so many days that the room's in a rut."

"Could be."

"Or Peter's set it to remain that way."

"Set it?"

"He may have got into the machinery and fixed something."

"Peter doesn't know machinery."

"He's a wise one for ten. That IQ of his—"

"Nevertheless—"

"Hello, Mom. Hello, Dad."

The Hadleys turned. Wendy and Peter were coming in the front door, cheeks like peppermint candy, eyes like bright blue agate marbles, a smell of ozone on their jumpers from their trip in the helicopter.

"You're just in time for supper," said both parents.

"We're full of strawberry ice cream and hot dogs," said the children, holding hands. "But we'll sit and watch."

"Yes, come tell us about the nursery," said George Hadley.

The brother and sister blinked at him and then at each other. "Nursery?"

"All about Africa and everything," said the father with false joviality.

"I don't understand," said Peter.

"Your mother and I were just traveling through Africa with rod and reel; Tom Swift and his Electric Lion," said George Hadley.

"There's no Africa in the nursery," said Peter simply.

"Oh, come now, Peter. We know better."

"I don't remember any Africa," said Peter to Wendy. "Do you?"

"No."

"Run see and come tell."

She obeyed.

"Wendy, come back here!" said George Hadley, but she was gone. The house lights followed her like a flock of fireflies. Too late, he realized he had forgotten to lock the nursery door after his last inspection.

"Wendy'll look and come tell us," said Peter.

"She doesn't have to tell *me*. I've seen it."

"I'm sure you're mistaken, Father."

"I'm not, Peter. Come along now."

But Wendy was back. "It's not Africa," she said breathlessly.

"We'll see about this," said George Hadley, and they all walked down the hall together and opened the nursery door.

There was a green, lovely forest, a lovely river, a purple mountain, high voices singing, and Rima, lovely and myste- rious, lurking in the trees with colorful flights of butterflies, like animated bouquets, lingering in her long hair. The African veldtland was gone. The lions were gone. Only Rima was here now, singing a song so beautiful that it brought tears to your eyes.

George Hadley looked in at the changed scene. "Go to bed," he said to the children.

They opened their mouths.

"You heard me," he said.

They went off to the air closet, where a wind sucked them like brown leaves up the flue to their slumber rooms.

George Hadley walked through the singing glade and picked up something that lay in the corner near where the lions had been. He walked slowly back to his wife.

"What is that?" she asked.

"An old wallet of mine," he said.

He showed it to her. The smell of hot grass was on it and the smell of a lion. There were drops of saliva on it, it had been chewed, and there were blood smears on both sides.

He closed the nursery door and locked it, tight.

In the middle of the night he was still awake and he knew his wife was awake. "Do you think Wendy changed it?" she said at last, in the dark room.

"Of course."

"Made it from a veldt into a forest and put Rima there instead of lions?"

"Yes."

"Why?"

"I don't know. But it's staying locked until I find out."

"How did your wallet get there?"

"I don't know anything," he said, "except that I'm beginning to be sorry we bought that room for the children. If children are neurotic at all, a room like that—"

"It's supposed to help them work off their neuroses in a healthful way."

"I'm starting to wonder." He stared at the ceiling.

"We've given the children everything they ever wanted. Is this our reward—secrecy, disobedience?"

"Who was it said, 'Children are carpets, they should be stepped on occasionally'? We've never lifted a hand. They're insufferable—let's admit it. They come and go when they like; they treat us as if *we* were offspring. They're spoiled and we're spoiled."

"They've been acting funny ever since you forbade them to take the rocket to New York a few months ago."

"They're not old enough to do that alone, I explained."

"Nevertheless, I've noticed they've been decidedly cool toward us since."

"I think I'll have David McClean come tomorrow morning to have a look at Africa."

"But it's not Africa now, it's *Green Mansions* country and Rima."

"I have a feeling it'll be Africa again before then."

A moment later they heard the screams.

Two screams. Two people screaming from downstairs. And then a roar of lions.

"Wendy and Peter aren't in their rooms," said his wife.

He lay in his bed with his beating heart. "No," he said. "They've broken into the nursery."

"Those screams—they sound familiar."

"Do they?"

"Yes, awfully."

And although their beds tried very hard, the two adults couldn't be rocked to sleep for another hour. A smell of cats was in the night air.

"Father?" said Peter.

"Yes."

Peter looked at his shoes. He never looked at his father anymore, nor at his mother. "You aren't going to lock up the nursery for good, are you?"

"That all depends."

"On what?" snapped Peter.

"On you and your sister. If you intersperse this Africa with a little variety—oh, Sweden perhaps, or Denmark or China—"

"I thought we were free to play as we wished."

"You are, within reasonable bounds."

"What's wrong with Africa, Father?"

"Oh, so now you admit you have been conjuring up Africa, do you?"

"I wouldn't want the nursery locked up," said Peter coldly. "Ever."

"Matter of fact, we're thinking of turning the whole house off for about a month. Live sort of a carefree one-for-all existence."

"That sounds dreadful! Would I have to tie my own shoes instead of letting the shoe tier do it? And brush my own teeth and comb my hair and give myself a bath?"

"It would be fun for a change, don't you think?"

"No, it would be horrid. I didn't like it when you took out the picture painter last month."

"That's because I wanted you to learn to paint all by yourself, son."

"I don't want to do anything but look and listen and smell; what else *is* there to do?"

"All right, go play in Africa."

"Will you shut off the house sometime soon?"

"We're considering it."

"I don't think you'd better consider it anymore, Father."

"I won't have any threats from my son!"

"Very well." And Peter strolled off to the nursery.

"Am I on time?" said David McClean.

"Breakfast?" asked George Hadley.

"Thanks, had some. What's the trouble?"

"David, you're a psychologist."

"I should hope so."

"Well, then, have a look at our nursery. You saw it a year ago when you dropped by; did you notice anything peculiar about it then?"

"Can't say I did; the usual violences, a tendency toward a slight paranoia here or there, usual in children because they feel persecuted by parents constantly, but, oh, really nothing."

They walked down the hall. "I locked the nursery up," explained the father, "and the children broke back into it during the night. I let them stay so they could form the patterns for you to see."

There was a terrible screaming from the nursery.

"There it is," said George Hadley. "See what you make of it."

They walked in on the children without rapping.

The screams had faded. The lions were feeding.

"Run outside a moment, children," said George Hadley. "No, don't change the mental combination. Leave the walls as they are. Get!"

With the children gone, the two men stood studying the lions clustered at a distance, eating with great relish whatever it was they had caught.

"I wish I knew what it was," said George Hadley. "Sometimes I can almost see. Do you think if I brought high-powered binoculars here and—"

David McClean laughed dryly. "Hardly." He turned to study all four walls. "How long has this been going on?"

"A little over a month."

"It certainly doesn't *feel* good."

"I want facts, not feelings."

"My dear George, a psychologist never saw a fact in his life. He only hears about feelings; vague things. This doesn't feel good, I tell you. Trust my hunches and my instincts. I have a nose for something bad. This is very bad. My advice to you is to have the whole damn room torn down and your children brought to me every day during the next year for treatment."

"Is it that bad?"

"I'm afraid so. One of the original uses of these nurseries was so that we could study the patterns left on the walls by the child's mind, study at our leisure, and help the child. In this case, however, the room has become a channel toward— destructive thoughts, instead of a release away from them."

"Didn't you sense this before?"

"I sensed only that you had spoiled your children more than most. And now you're letting them down in some way. What way?"

"I wouldn't let them go to New York."

"What else?"

"I've taken a few machines from the house and threatened them, a month ago, with closing up the nursery unless they did their homework. I did close it for a few days to show I meant business."

"Ah, ha!"

"Does that mean anything?"

"Everything. Where before they had a Santa Claus now they have a Scrooge. Children prefer Santas. You've let this room and this house replace you and your wife in your children's affections. This room is their mother and father, far more important in their lives than their real parents. And now you come along and want to shut it off. No wonder there's hatred here. You can feel it coming out of the sky. Feel that sun. George, you'll have to change your life. Like too many others, you've built it around creature comforts. Why, you'd starve tomorrow if something went wrong in your kitchen. You wouldn't know how to tap an egg. Nevertheless, turn everything off. Start new. It'll take time. But we'll make good children out of bad in a year, wait and see."

"But won't the shock be too much for the children, shutting the room up abruptly, for good?"

"I don't want them going any deeper into this, that's all."

The lions were finished with their red feast.

The lions were standing on the edge of the clearing watching the two men.

"Now *I'm* feeling persecuted," said McClean. "Let's get out of here. I never have cared for these damned rooms. Make me nervous."

"The lions look real, don't they?" said George Hadley. "I don't suppose there's any way—"

"What?"

"—that they could *become* real?"

"Not that I know."

"Some flaw in the machinery, a tampering or something?"

"No."

They went to the door.

"I don't imagine the room will like being turned off," said the father.

"Nothing ever likes to die—even a room."

"I wonder if it hates me for wanting to switch it off?"

"Paranoia is thick around here today," said David McClean. "You can follow it like a spoor. Hello." He bent and picked up a bloody scarf. "This yours?"

"No." George Hadley's face was rigid. "It belongs to Lydia."

They went to the fuse box together and threw the switch that killed the nursery.

The two children were in hysterics. They screamed and pranced and threw things. They yelled and sobbed and swore and jumped at the furniture.

RAY BRADBURY

"You can't do that to the nursery, you can't!"

"Now, children."

The children flung themselves onto a couch, weeping.

"George," said Lydia Hadley, "turn on the nursery, just for a few moments. You can't be so abrupt."

"No."

"You can't be so cruel."

"Lydia, it's off, and it stays off. And the whole damn house dies as of here and now. The more I see of the mess we've put ourselves in, the more it sickens me. We've been contemplating our mechanical, electronic navels for too long. My God, how we need a breath of honest air!"

And he marched about the house turning off the voice clocks, the stoves, the heaters, the shoe shiners, the shoe lacers, the body scrubbers and swabbers and massagers, and every other machine he could put his hand to.

The house was full of dead bodies, it seemed. It felt like a mechanical cemetery. So silent. None of the humming hidden energy of machines waiting to function at the tap of a button.

"Don't let them do it!" wailed Peter at the ceiling, as if he was talking to the house, the nursery. "Don't let Father kill everything." He turned to his father. "Oh, I hate you!"

"Insults won't get you anywhere."

"I wish you were dead!"

"We were, for a long while. Now we're going to really start living. Instead of being handled and massaged, we're going to *live.*"

Wendy was still crying and Peter joined her again. "Just a moment, just one moment, just another moment of nursery," they wailed.

"Oh, George," said the wife, "it can't hurt."

104

"All right—all right, if they'll only just shut up. One minute, mind you, and then off forever."

"Daddy, Daddy, Daddy!" sang the children, smiling with wet faces.

"And then we're going on a vacation. David McClean is coming back in half an hour to help us move out and get to the airport. I'm going to dress. You turn the nursery on for a minute, Lydia, just a minute, mind you."

And the three of them went babbling off while he let himself be vacuumed upstairs through the air flue and set about dressing himself. A minute later Lydia appeared.

"I'll be glad when we get away," she sighed.

"Did you leave them in the nursery?"

"I wanted to dress too. Oh, that horrid Africa. What can they see in it?"

"Well, in five minutes we'll be on our way to Iowa. Lord, how did we ever get in this house? What prompted us to buy a nightmare?"

"Pride, money, foolishness."

"I think we'd better get downstairs before those kids get engrossed with those damned beasts again."

Just then they heard the children calling, "Daddy, Mommy, come quick—quick!"

They went downstairs in the air flue and ran down the hall. The children were nowhere in sight. "Wendy? Peter!"

They ran into the nursery. The veldtland was empty save for the lions waiting, looking at them. "Peter, Wendy?"

The door slammed.

"Wendy, Peter!"

George Hadley and his wife whirled and ran back to the door.

"Open the door!" cried George Hadley, trying the knob. "Why, they've locked it from the outside! Peter!" He beat at the door. "Open up!"

He heard Peter's voice outside, against the door.

"Don't let them switch off the nursery and the house," he was saying.

Mr. and Mrs. George Hadley beat at the door. "Now, don't be ridiculous, children. It's time to go. Mr. McClean'll be here in a minute and . . ."

And then they heard the sounds.

The lions on three sides of them, in the yellow veldt grass, padding through the dry straw, rumbling and roaring in their throats.

The lions.

Mr. Hadley looked at his wife and they turned and looked back at the beasts edging slowly forward, crouching, tails stiff.

Mr. and Mrs. Hadley screamed.

And suddenly they realized why those other screams had sounded familiar.

"Well, here I am," said David McClean in the nursery doorway. "Oh, hello." He stared at the two children seated in the center of the open glade eating a little picnic lunch. Beyond them was the water hole and the yellow veldtland; above was the hot sun. He began to perspire. "Where are your father and mother?"

The children looked up and smiled. "Oh, they'll be here directly."

"Good, we must get going." At a distance Mr. McClean saw the lions fighting and clawing and then quieting down to feed in silence under the shady trees.

He squinted at the lions with his hand up to his eyes.

Now the lions were done feeding. They moved to the water hole to drink.

A shadow flickered over Mr. McClean's hot face. Many shadows flickered. The vultures were dropping down the blazing sky.

"A cup of tea?" asked Wendy in the silence.

A LIKELY PLACE

Paula Fox

1

Everyone wanted to help Lewis. That's why he was thinking of running away.

But where could he go? He only had thirty-five cents left from his birthday present. His two Canadian dimes didn't count unless he could get as far as Canada.

Lewis was lying in bed watching the reflections of car lights move across his ceiling. He was thinking that if he could just remember the difference between *there* and *their* school wouldn't be so bad, when his mother came into his room.

"Are you still awake, Lewis?" she asked.

"Sort of," he said.

"Is there something on your mind, dear?"

What *was* on his mind? Lewis wondered. Skin, then brownish hair, then a woolen cap he had taken to wearing even when the weather was warm.

"Why, Lewis! You're still wearing that hat!" his mother exclaimed. "In bed, Lewis!"

"I forgot to take it off," he answered, which was only half true. He didn't especially want to explain that wearing the hat made him feel everything inside his head was in the right place.

"Well . . ." his mother said, hesitating at the door, "I think you should try to sleep."

He listened to his mother's footsteps going on down the hall, then he got up and walked over to his fish tank. The fish had been supplied by his parents to give him something to take care of so he could become responsible. They bored him to death.

When Lewis awoke the next morning, his youngest cousin was sitting on his bed. Lewis knew it must be Saturday. One Saturday every month his uncle and aunt and cousin came to visit.

"Where'd you get that hat?" asked his cousin.

"It's just a hat," said Lewis.

"A sleeping hat," said the cousin.

Lewis got up and began to get dressed. His clothes were in a heap where he had left them. His cousin watched as Lewis untangled a shoelace from a belt buckle and a shirt sleeve from a pants leg.

"You'll probably end up at Charlie Flocker's Farm," his cousin said.

"What's that?" asked Lewis.

"Oh, a place for people who hang their clothes on the floor and who sit down and don't do anything all day," replied the cousin.

"Who told you that?" asked Lewis.

"My mother told me," said his cousin. "And her mother told her, and her mother's mother—"

"Stop!" shouted Lewis. "Just tell me, what do they do there?"

The cousin crossed his eyes.

Lewis considered asking his own mother about Charlie Flocker. Probably she would say, "Oh, Lewis!" and give him an oatmeal cookie.

Lewis and his cousin went off to the kitchen to get some breakfast. His aunt and uncle and mother and father were drinking coffee at the kitchen table. They all looked up.

"I found the slipper you lost last month, Lewis," said his mother. "It was under the refrigerator."

"Lewis, do you have a plan for those batteries which are soaking in your spare fishbowl?" asked his father. "Because if you don't, I'll just remove them. A pity to stain the glass so."

That morning he and his cousin were taken to the museum. It was one of many places Lewis was taken to, even when he didn't care to go: the zoo, the playground, the beach, plays, concerts, ballets, museums.

Lewis's cousin found a big glass case full of swords. While they were deciding which ones they would like to have, Lewis's aunt called out, "Lewis, do look at this nice little sphinx! Imagine! It's three thousand years old!"

Then his mother called out, "Lewis, come and see this statue of a Roman senator. Doesn't it look like your uncle?"

He wondered why they left his cousin alone. Maybe it was because his cousin was still little. Lewis leaned up against a column until a museum guard scowled and motioned to him to move. His father hurried over.

"Are you all right?" asked his father.

"Fine," said Lewis. If he could have one wish it would be to make people stop asking him how he felt—or telling him how he felt. "You must feel embarrassed because you spell so poorly," his teacher would say. "You must feel lonely on a rainy day like this with no one to play with," a friend of his mother would say. "It's too bad you live in the city where you only have a dirty, dinky playground to run around in," an absolute stranger would say. Lewis could have made a list a mile long of all the things people had told him he was feeling.

Just before his aunt and uncle left the museum to go home, his cousin whispered to him, "If you have a book and act like you're reading it, it's easier."

That night he took a book from the shelf, and while he was lying in bed looking at it, a hand turned it over to see the title. It was his mother's hand, but his father's voice said, "Hm . . . well . . . I see . . . uh-huh . . . well, well!"

Lewis spent most of Sunday thinking about running away. He wondered if anyone guessed. The doorman of the building across the street always seemed to be watching for him. He had heard of mind readers. Maybe the doorman was one.

His mother and father were walking back and forth in the living room exchanging sections of the Sunday paper. Lewis went out on the service stairs of the building to play solitaire. He liked it on the stairs. When the handymen who fixed things ran up and down from floor to floor, the noise was thunderous but Lewis didn't mind. The king of hearts in his deck of cards had a large sooty heel print where one of the handymen had stepped on it. He could have erased the print with his gum eraser if he hadn't lost it.

The next morning as he passed the doorman on his way to catch the school bus, the doorman called out, "Hello, kid. That's the ticket, kid! Get yourself educated!"

Why would the doorman say that to him, Lewis asked himself, unless he suspected that Lewis was up to something? Something like running away?

When he got to school, Lewis suddenly remembered the test the class was having the first thing that morning. But he had forgotten the name of the capital of Honduras. He stood in the corridor, knowing he had been marked absent. He was leaning against the wall, trying to think what to do, when the school principal walked up and put his arm around his shoulders.

"Lewis, you should be in class," he said.

"I know it," Lewis replied.

"We are trying to help children, Lewis," said the principal. "But they have to try, too. Isn't that so?"

Lewis had heard some other questions like that one. "It's raining out, isn't it?" or "It's time for you to go to bed, isn't it?" or "Tomatoes are good for you, aren't they?" If he said *no* to any of these questions, grownups would look dizzy.

The principal led Lewis into the classroom. The principal smiled at the teacher, who smiled back. Lewis didn't smile at anybody. He couldn't even remember where Honduras was.

When he got home that afternoon, his mother said she had something to tell him. In a few days, she said, it would be May, time for the annual trip to Chicago to visit relatives.

"We'll only be gone for a week," she said.

"Okay," said Lewis.

"You'll like Miss Fitchlow who is going to take care of you," she said.

"All right," said Lewis.

"Next year, we might even take you," his mother said. "If your schoolwork gets better."

He started for his room.

"Oh, Lewis, your three friends are waiting for you. Outside on the service stairs."

Lewis was glad to hear they were there and ran to the hall closet to get the old army blanket for them to sit on, because the stairs were cold. If they got cold they wouldn't stay to hear the ghost stories he read to them.

"Lewis! Wait!" his mother said. "How old are Henry and Betty Anne and Thomas?"

"Different ages," said Lewis.

"Oh, Lewis! I mean their average age."

"They're all around seven," Lewis answered.

"And you're going to be ten soon," his mother said. "Don't you think they're a little young for you? Wouldn't you rather play with children your own age?"

Lewis shrugged. He knew his mother was smiling only because she wanted him to do something different from what he was going to do.

"Are your friends all the same age?" he asked.

"That's not polite, Lewis," his mother replied.

"I was only asking," he said.

He did like to read to the children. They often waited for him in the afternoon. Henry usually had an apple and Betty Anne and Thomas had a box of animal crackers. Until his eyes got used to the light in the service stairs he could hardly see anything except their eyes. They reminded him of a family of pandas. They each sat on their own step, squinched up against the wall, looking to see which book he had brought with him. The only objection he had to reading to them was that they liked to hear the same story over and over again. He had read *The Monkey's Paw* a dozen times. They particularly liked him to screech or moan or squeak like a door with rusty hinges at the exciting parts.

When Lewis's mother called out from the kitchen to see if everyone was all right, Henry shouted back, "Super!" Lewis wished he could get the hang of answering grownups. It seemed to him that everyone knew how to manage this problem except him.

On Tuesday, at school, the whole class had a recorder lesson. But Lewis had to have an extra one. He hadn't yet learned the school song or the special piece his class was to play on their recorders for assembly. Miss Mowdith, the music teacher, said that Lewis was throwing the whole class off key.

"I think, Lewis," she said, "that you must be hearing the music of outer space. I never heard a G like that in my entire life! My dear boy! If we could amplify that note of yours over a public-address system, all the mice living in this city would hit the road!"

So that afternoon Lewis went to Miss Mowdith's apartment for his special lesson. The two rooms were filled with musical instruments. Even in the kitchen, there were piccolos. A blue-eyed cat was sitting on a harpsichord.

"The cat bites people," Miss Mowdith said as Lewis reached up a hand to pet it.

Then Lewis played his G. The cat jumped a foot in the air and ran for cover.

"Oh!" exclaimed Miss Mowdith. "What shall we ever do with you?"

That, Lewis gathered, was the problem. Even Henry had complained yesterday that Lewis's screeches weren't as scary as they used to be.

On Thursday he handed in his weekly composition, and no sooner had his teacher looked at it than she dropped it on her desk.

"Lewis, you must learn to spell *their*. What will happen to you if you can't tell the difference between *there* and *their*?"

What *would* happen? Lewis wondered, as he wrote *their* fifty times. He was writing out the words so they formed a design like a snake on the lined paper. The teacher looked over his shoulder. "Lewis, you must learn the difference between a drawing class and a spelling exercise."

He put a note on the teacher's desk in which he wrote that her elbows looked like clam shells. He didn't sign it, but she seemed to know whom it was from.

"Not everyone in this world can have beautiful elbows," she said to him that afternoon.

That evening his father, who had heard about Lewis's spelling difficulties, said, "I should think a ten-year-old boy would be able to spell *their*."

"I'm nine," said Lewis.

"Going on ten," said his father. "Maybe I can help you."

But Lewis spelled *their* instantly and correctly.

"Any other words bothering you?" asked his father as he picked up Lewis's marbles from the living room floor and handed them to him.

"Not yet," said Lewis.

"That's not what I heard," said his father.

"Heard," repeated Lewis, "h-e-a-r-d."

"All right, Lewis. That will do!" said his father.

Lewis would have liked Fridays to disappear from the week. But then, he supposed, he would have to have the weekly spelling test on Thursday. But to his surprise he spelled *their* correctly that morning. The teacher announced to the class that Lewis had, at last, learned the word. Lewis felt rather good about the whole thing except that he wished his classmates hadn't clapped so loudly.

Later his teacher took him aside, reminding him that the spring reports would be due soon. She asked him what he was really interested in.

"Pygmies," said Lewis.

"Don't be funny," she said. Lewis looked down at his shoes. He had drawn a face on the toe of one with a marking pen. It was his right shoe. He had trouble remembering which was right and which was left. The face reminded him.

"Perhaps you're serious," the teacher said. "Would you like to make your report on pygmies? We're delighted you're interested in something."

Pygmies did interest him. He had seen a picture of a pygmy bridge in a magazine. It had been made from vines and then slung over a stream somewhere in Africa. There were several pygmies standing in the middle of the bridge with their arms around one another. They were all smiling.

"Could I do a report on something else?" Lewis asked. He wanted to keep the pygmies for himself. He didn't care to write all about the population of the pygmies or what they ate and what they learned in school or how they made a living. He didn't want to cut out and paste pictures of pygmies on white paper and put a cover around his report and read it to the class.

The teacher sighed. "Well. . . . Do a report on something," she said.

That very evening his father asked him what he liked best.

"A pygmy bridge," Lewis said, because it had been on his mind all day.

His father sighed too. "I don't understand you, Lewis," he said. His mother gave him a cookie and said they would bring him back a nice present from Chicago.

That's the way things were with Lewis.

2

As soon as it was May the weather seemed to change and grow warmer. Cats came out from behind garbage cans and wandered down the streets. The trees began to bloom. The doorman across the street unbuttoned his jacket, leaned against the wall, and went to sleep standing up. Young flies flew through the classroom, and a bee crawled in one morning and swooped across the desks while all the girls screamed.

Lewis's mother and father would soon be leaving for Chicago.

"A little change of routine," his father said. "It'll be a change for you, too, Lewis," he added.

Lewis wasn't interested in going to Chicago but he didn't want to stay home either. He hadn't met Miss Fitchlow yet. His mother said she was very nice. What could that mean? He hoped she wouldn't be like some of the other babysitters he had had. Mrs. Carmichael, for instance, had worn fat, purple slippers and had followed him around all day, and had even sat next to his bed at night until he had pretended to fall asleep. Mrs. Carmichael had hummed to herself all day long, always just one note. Perhaps that's where he had learned his special G.

Or Miss Fitchlow might be like Jake Elderberry, who sat on evenings when his parents went to the movies, and whose hair fell over his eyes and who thought he saw things behind the curtains. Or worst of all, she might be like Miss Bender, who weighed all the food she intended to eat on a little scale, and who washed everything a hundred times and who practically fell out the window scaring away the birds because, she said, they carried deadly germs in their feathers.

On Saturday morning while his parents were packing, Lewis went out for a walk. The sun was warm. He passed many baby carriages and children on tricycles. At the entrance to the park he saw dozens of dogs running around with their ears and tails up. They looked very busy. As he was watching them, he noticed a fat woman walking right toward him. She wobbled.

"Hello, honey," she said. "Knock 'em dead!" she added seriously, and her words ran together as though the sun was melting them.

He stared at her as she passed him and wobbled on down the street. Then, because he wanted to see what she would do next, he ran after her until people began to look at him and scowl.

"Running boys should do without their suppers!" croaked an old man, waving his cane at Lewis as he ran by. Finally he couldn't see the lady anymore. He went back to the park entrance. He hadn't been in the park without his father or his mother. In another year, his father said, he would be allowed to go by himself if he had gotten to be a responsible boy by that time. It was, after all, a very big park. Lewis couldn't even see over the trees to the other side, where the river was. There was a zoo in it somewhere. There were lakes and paths and big rocks. Lewis thought that there must be a cave or two. He hoped he might be able to live in one for a while.

When he got back to the apartment, his parents were standing in the hall with their suitcases beside them. A tall, thin lady with a freckled face and reddish hair was there with them.

"This is Miss Fitchlow, Lewis," said his mother. "She has our number."

Miss Fitchlow laughed. She sounded like a horse. Lewis noticed his mother looked quickly at his father. Then his parents hugged him and reminded him of all the things he needed and all the things he should do as well as all the things he shouldn't do. Then they left.

"Say, pal, you've got a face on your left shoe," said Miss Fitchlow as they were standing in the hall.

"It's on my right shoe," Lewis said.

"Right you are!" Miss Fitchlow cried. "I ought to know that by now. Come with me! I'll show you something."

Lewis followed her into the living room, where Miss Fitchlow sank down instantly to the floor, her feet arranged in a peculiar way, crossed, each foot pointing straight up.

"Lotus position," she said. "Keep your back straight. Breathe deeply. Be quiet about it. Think nothing. Marvelous for the appetite. Do you like yogurt? Some hate it. I brought my own

119

brand. You can try it. Also pumpkin seeds. But honey is the greatest! What's the matter? Can't get your legs crossed? What do you expect? It takes time to learn, like everything else."

Lewis fell over backwards.

"What's this for besides appetite?" Lewis asked.

"Anything at all," Miss Fitchlow replied.

He ate a chop for dinner. Miss Fitchlow sloshed around a big bowl of yogurt. It tasted queer to him—like undecided milk.

"How about some nuts?" she asked.

They ate nuts until there was a big pile of shells on the kitchen table.

"Something on your mind?" she asked. "So have I." But she didn't ask him what it was, or tell him what she was thinking about.

He decided to ask her a question he had been turning over for a week or so.

"Did you ever hear of Charlie Flocker?" he asked.

She rested her chin on her hand. "Charlie Flocker? Let's see. Say, I knew a Charlie Flocker in Bombay. He was there to study the rope trick. I don't think he ever could manage it. It's pretty tough to just disappear."

"Bombay?" asked Lewis.

"India," she said.

"He runs a farm," Lewis said.

"Not the Charlie I knew," said Miss Fitchlow. "He couldn't run a scooter."

"Maybe there're two of them," said Lewis.

"Possible, but not probable," said Miss Fitchlow.

"He runs this place for people who don't do anything," Lewis said.

"That's for me!" shouted Miss Fitchlow and laughed her horse laugh. Then she began to wash the dishes.

"I hate to dry," she said. "You dry, pal."

"I don't know how," Lewis said.

She handed him a wet plate and a towel. "Figure it out," she said.

He dropped one fork and when it clanged on the kitchen floor, Miss Fitchlow did a little dancing, snapping her fingers together and rolling her eyes.

The next morning Lewis found Miss Fitchlow in the living room lying between two chairs, her feet on one, her head on the other, the rest of her in-between.

"Pretty good, eh?" she said. "Took me years to learn this one. You can start your breakfast. I have another two minutes to go before I can get up."

Lewis went to the kitchen but there was nothing on the table. He drank a whole can of apricot juice and toasted an English muffin, which he ate with peanut butter on it.

"How was it?" asked Miss Fitchlow from the door. She looked a little taller. He wondered if her morning exercise had stretched her.

"It was okay," said Lewis.

"What have you in mind for today?" she asked.

"I thought I'd go to the park," he said, hoping his parents hadn't told Miss Fitchlow he wasn't responsible yet.

"Pretty good," she said. "Cover the peanut butter. It'll get dry as a bone. No point in that."

He did.

"Not that fresh peanuts aren't better," she added.

The dogs in the park were not so busy today. Some of them were asleep, stretched out beneath the trees with their tails curled around them so they looked like neat packages. Lewis walked through the entrance. He would have been worried if he hadn't been so excited. He could just imagine his father

121

smiling as he said, "Why, Lewis! Don't you remember that we asked you not to go into the park?"

Then he saw a small snake curling through the grass. He leaped for it. It wound itself around his wrist. A lady who was passing by uttered a little screech and hurried on. A man walked up to him.

"What have you there?" he asked.

"A snake," said Lewis.

"So I see," the man said, "but one must do better than that. It is known as DeKay's snake. Notice the chestnut color. Note the black dots along its sides."

The snake slid off Lewis's arm and disappeared beneath a bush.

"Easy come, easy go," said the man. Lewis walked on.

Everything in the world seemed to have a name.

He came to a fork in the path and, looking down at his shoes, turned right. Soon he came to a small square enclosed by trees, with benches all around a few yards of gravel. An old man was sitting alone on a bench. He wore a high, black hat and had on gloves. There was a large umbrella furled across his lap. Lewis observed him for a while. The old man was talking to himself. Although he spoke in a loud, clear voice, the words were in a language which Lewis didn't understand.

A boy zipped through the square on a bicycle. Lewis jumped back. The old man looked up.

"Too fast!" said the old man. "Square wheels would have changed history." Lewis wasn't sure to whom he was speaking.

"You got a bicycle, too?" asked the old man. Lewis looked around quickly. But there was no one in the square except himself and the old man. He shook his head.

"I only wish I had such a bicycle," the old man said, sighing. "I'd ride it like a devil. Ride it, ride it all the way home!"

Lewis looked at the umbrella so the old man couldn't tell that he was surprised.

"Who can tell?" said the old man. "It might rain."

Another mind reader, thought Lewis, and he started to leave the square.

"Wait!" cried the old man. "Don't you want to know where my home is? Have you no curiosity?"

Lewis halted. If he walked away, the old man might ask him where he was going. He might even tell him he shouldn't be in the park.

"Barcelona!" shouted the old man. "And I'll tell you something. If I could ride a bicycle in the first place, I could ride it across the Atlantic Ocean in the second place."

"Is that the capital of Honduras?" Lewis asked.

"Honduras!" exclaimed the old man. "Barcelona in Honduras," he repeated as if astonished. "Why—it's in Spain, dear friend. Come over here and sit down. I must tell you a thing or two."

Lewis sat down on the bench next to the old man.

"It is a large city, very splendid, on the Mediterranean Sea. Ships come to its harbor from all over the world, even from Honduras. In the middle of the streets there are *ramblas*. On those splendid *ramblas* a person can walk at any time of the day or night and nobody will knock him down with a car. In the afternoons after my work was done, I had a cup of chocolate so thick it had to be eaten with a spoon. Often I think to myself—what has happened, Emilio? Boys on bicycles make my brains rattle, and instead of chocolate in the afternoons, I sit here on this bench and try to compose myself and write a letter, and when it is too cold to sit here, I sit in my room and try to write this same letter."

"Who are you writing to?" asked Lewis.

The old man scowled. "To my son-in-law who married my daughter, Preciosa."

"Where does he live?" asked Lewis.

"In the same house I am," replied the old man.

"Can't you just tell him?" Lewis asked.

"Can you tell a rock? No! I will write. Then I must go home to Barcelona," said the old man.

"All right," said Lewis.

"It's all wrong," said the old man. "I been here three years. Observe my English! Beautiful! But I can't write it. What kind of mad language is it? You see a word and it's nothing like the way you say it. Sometimes I jump up and down on the newspapers and Preciosa comes running and explains to me the stupid word I cannot understand because of this crazy spelling. The sound and the writing are not even cousins. In my language, it's intelligent. My name is Madruga. Spell it!"

"Me?" asked Lewis.

"You," said the old man.

Lewis spelled it.

"Perfect! You see?" asked the old man. "Even a person who does not speak can spell. What is your name?"

"Lewis."

The old man spelled: "L-u-i-s."

"No," said Lewis.

"Try another," said the old man.

"Cough," said Lewis.

"Ah!" exclaimed the old man. "Watch! C-o-f."

"Wrong," said Lewis.

"Naturally," said the old man. "Because it is unreasonable, English. What can you expect?"

"Where did you have the chocolate?" asked Lewis.

"In the café," said the old man. "At a table beneath a small umbrella, out on the sidewalk where I could watch the people walking pleasantly on the *ramblas*. But now I have neither chocolate nor work. My son-in-law won't permit me. I am extraordinarily skilled. I make beautiful shoes, everything by hand. But he says I drop things. I have never dropped anything in my life. He says, 'Go read the newspapers.' What is in the newspapers? News. Nothing."

"What do you do?" asked Lewis.

"I come to the park and sit on this bench and think about this letter which I cannot write. I sit and sit. Then I go home and sit in my room. Then it is supper at a barbaric hour, 5:30. My son-in-law doesn't eat. How can he? He is watching me all the time. 'Pa,' he says, 'you are about to drop your spoon.'"

"What's his name?" asked Lewis.

"Charlie," replied the old man, looking sad.

"Charlie Flocker?" asked Lewis.

"What's that?" asked the old man.

"Nothing," said Lewis. Then he asked, "What's the letter for?"

"For telling Charlie what I think. Also my plans. He thinks I am too old to have plans," replied the old man.

They were silent for a little while.

"I suppose," the old man said at last, "that you can write this insane language, English?"

"Sometimes," said Lewis.

"Ah, I understand," said the old man. "It is like having fits, no?"

Lewis nodded.

"Would you do me the great favor of writing this letter?" asked the old man. He looked at Lewis with a serious expression. "I will tell it to you," he said, "and you will spell."

"Okay," said Lewis. "But I make mistakes."

"Think nothing of it," said the old man. "Could we begin now? I have paper and pencil in my pocket."

"I was going to look for a cave," said Lewis.

The old man looked disappointed.

"But I can do it tomorrow," said Lewis.

"I am very good at caves," said the old man eagerly. "And I can help you. That will be in exchange for the letter."

"All right," Lewis said.

The old man reached into his pocket and took out a pad of paper and a short yellow pencil.

"My esteemed son-in-law Charles," he began.

Lewis looked up at him. "How about 'Dear Charlie'?" he asked.

"Ah, that's better," said the old man. "Customs are different everywhere. Now, write: 'Sometimes I ask myself what am I? An old chair to gather dust in the corner? Me? A skilled shoemaker?'"

"Wait!" said Lewis. "You're going too fast."

The old man folded his hands over his umbrella and waited until Lewis was finished writing.

"Here's what I wrote," said Lewis shortly. "'Dear Charlie, I don't want to sit in a corner. I want to make some shoes.'"

The old man smiled for the first time. A gold tooth shone in his mouth. "Very good," he said. "Now—"

But he was interrupted by the appearance in the square of a large man in a green jacket. Lewis wondered whose hat he was wearing. It couldn't have been his own.

"Pa!" cried the man. "Pressy's got a big Sunday dinner all ready and here you are, stuck to that bench as usual. The spuds are burned and the peas are as hard as pebbles. Come on home now before something else happens!"

The old man whispered to Lewis behind his hand. "You heard? *Pressy!* My poor daughter!"

"Move, Pa!" said the man. "You ought to play with people your own age!"

The old man shouted rapidly in the same language Lewis had heard him speak when he first came to the square.

"Cut the cackle!" said Charlie. "Let's make time!"

The old man rose slowly to his feet and bowed to Lewis. "Perhaps we can continue tomorrow," he said gravely.

"It has to be later because of school," Lewis explained.

"At your convenience," said the old man.

"Pa!" bawled the large man.

"After three," Lewis said hurriedly.

"I will be here with the nothing newspaper," said the old man, and he twirled his umbrella and began to walk away.

"*Adiós,*" he called back over his shoulder.

When Lewis walked into his apartment, Miss Fitchlow was standing on her head in a corner of the hall.

"Good for the brains," she said.

3

Lewis looked at the classroom clock only twice during the day. Each time, he was surprised to see how far the hour hand had advanced.

It was a strange Monday. He hardly knew he was in school because he was thinking so hard about old Mr. Madruga and about how he must finish all his work so he would not be kept in after school.

While he was looking up the word *shoemaker* in the classroom dictionary (in case he should have to use it in Mr. Madruga's letter), he found a number of other words he had not seen before. He learned, for example, that *shoo* was a sound used to frighten birds away, and that a *shogun* was a Japanese ruler.

"Why, Lewis!" cried his teacher. "You're using the dictionary!"

Lewis muttered "shoo!" under his breath.

"What?" asked the teacher.

"Spanish is easier to spell," he said.

"So it is," she agreed.

"What's your hurry, kid?" shouted the doorman as Lewis raced past him on his way home.

Miss Fitchlow was in the kitchen making carrot pudding.

"In case you want to see in the dark," said Miss Fitchlow, pointing to the pudding, "this guarantees it. Takes a bit of getting used to, though. How about a taste?"

"Wow!" said Lewis after he had taken a bite.

He waited for her to ask him what had happened in school. Perhaps she didn't really know where he had been most of the day.

"I was in school," he said.

"Ah!" said Miss Fitchlow. "The old daily double."

"I've got to go to the park now," he said.

"Okay," said Miss Fitchlow.

"What are you going to do?" Lewis asked.

"Meditate," she replied.

"What's that?" he asked.

"Clean out the attic," she said.

He thought about attics all the way to the square in the park. He thought of trunks and spider webs and old birdcages, the kind he had seen in his cousin's attic. Miss Fitchlow reminded

him of agreeable things even though he didn't always understand what she was talking about.

Mr. Madruga was sitting on the same bench, his umbrella
resting between his knees, a folded newspaper beside him.
Lewis thought he was asleep. Then the old man looked up.

"Oho!" said Mr. Madruga. "My dear friend, I've made you
something." He held out a bird made from newspaper. It was
very small and had many paper feathers. It rested lightly on
Lewis's palm.

"Thank you," he said.

"It's nothing," said the old man. "First, we will look for a
cave."

Lewis was happy because Mr. Madruga had remembered.

They walked away from the square and down a path. They
passed a duck pond. The ducks were gathered around an old
lady, through whose fingers grains of corn trickled.

"My ducks!" she cried as they walked by.

"Splendid!" said Mr. Madruga loudly. He whispered to
Lewis, "Personally, I don't care for ducks."

The path they were following wound up a hill. At the top,
where there were no trees, only a few gray rocks, they found a
man staring up at the sun. They watched him a minute.

"What are you doing, please?" asked Mr. Madruga politely.

"I'm teaching myself to look at the sun," the man said.

"I can see the sun," Lewis said.

"No, you can't," said the man. "No one can see it. It's much
too bright. But in a few days, I will be able to see it. Then I'll
write a book. I'll call it, 'The Sun and I.' Or even better, 'I and
the Sun.'" Suddenly he turned to look at them. "I can't see you
yet," he said. "If you wait a minute until my eyes adjust, I'll
describe my plan to you."

Mr. Madruga and Lewis tiptoed down the other side of the hill. When they looked back, the man had resumed his former position and was staring straight up at the sky.

"Can you see the sun?" asked Lewis.

"In a way," replied Mr. Madruga. "But I prefer to see the ground." Then he cried, "Look out for the infants!"

Just in time, Lewis saw two babies crawling at high speed directly toward him. Behind them, huffing and panting, came a lady in a white uniform.

"Gertrude! Matthew! This is positively the worst you've ever been. Come back! Come back at once!" she cried.

But the babies kept right on going, so Lewis had to jump off the path to get out of their way.

"Devils!" muttered the lady as she passed them. Mr. Madruga was laughing so hard that he had to lean on his umbrella. Lewis began to laugh too.

"Maybe they'll escape," he said.

"No, no," said Mr. Madruga, wiping his eyes. "They won't escape. But they go very fast, no?"

"Will we find a cave soon?" asked Lewis.

"In time," said Mr. Madruga. "An empty cave is the most difficult thing of all to find." Then he turned off the path, holding back the branches of some thick bushes so that Lewis could follow him.

"Why are we going here?" asked Lewis.

"It's a likely place," answered Mr. Madruga.

How different the park looked here! No paths, no baskets for litter, no benches, no people. It was almost like the country. They walked through a small meadow of fresh spring grass. Ahead of them was another hill, but this one had no paths, and the rock faces were steep and smooth. Lewis ran

130

ahead. Almost immediately he saw a cave opening. It was dark and jagged but wide enough even for Mr. Madruga. Lewis peered inside.

"Occupied!" shouted a voice.

"Inhabited!" shouted another.

"Positively filled to capacity!" cried a third.

Lewis sprang back.

"That was full," he reported to Mr. Madruga, who had waited for him in the meadow.

"There will be more," said Mr. Madruga.

The next cave was too small for Lewis to get his head in and look around. The third cave was full of water. "For that one," said Mr. Madruga, "we would need a boat."

"We'll never find one," said Lewis, feeling discouraged.

"There!" said Mr. Madruga, pointing with his umbrella right in front of them. All Lewis could see was a tangle of vines.

"Lift them!" said the old man. Lewis pushed the vines away.

"What have you found?" asked Mr. Madruga.

"A big, empty cave," said Lewis.

It was large enough at the entrance for both of them to enter at the same time. There was a low ledge near the entrance upon which Mr. Madruga spread his newspaper. He sat down and waited while Lewis explored the cave.

Ten long strides took Lewis to the back wall. There he found a candle stub stuck into a soup can. He also found one black shoe with its laces. He must remember to look for someone wearing only one shoe on his way home. Underneath some dead leaves, he found a small, slightly damp booklet. The title was *Mosquito Control in Southeastern Delaware.*

Lewis returned to Mr. Madruga with the candle and the booklet.

Mr. Madruga took a kitchen match from his pocket and after lighting it with his thumbnail, lit the candle. Then he took out the notebook in which Lewis had started the letter to Charlie yesterday. Lewis put the paper bird down on the ledge between them.

They didn't really need the candle, because daylight was pouring in through the mouth of the cave. But it was nice to see the flame flicker in the light breeze.

"Shall we continue?" asked Mr. Madruga.

"Ready," said Lewis.

"You are content with your cave?" asked Mr. Madruga.

"Yes," said Lewis.

"In my country," said Mr. Madruga, "only the best dancers and the best singers live in caves."

"With furniture?" asked Lewis.

"With everything. Everything," answered the old man. Then he said, "Use the book you found for a little desk."

Lewis held up the pencil to show he was ready.

"Without work, I am nothing, nothing, an empty valise!" cried Mr. Madruga. "Charlie! You have stopped me from looking for work. You tell me to 'take it easy,' and I ask myself, what does this mean—"

"Wait!" cried Lewis.

"I was carried away by my feelings," explained Mr. Madruga.

"Is this all right?" asked Lewis after thinking and writing a few minutes. Then he read, " 'You won't let me look for work.' "

"Yes, yes," said Mr. Madruga. "He even says I must not carry my umbrella. He says it's old-fashioned. Is rain old-fashioned? Also, it is pleasant to lean on. Imagine! He puts food into my mouth, turns out my light at night, and holds my arm when we walk as if I were going to fall down on my knees!"

Mr. Madruga stood up and flourished his umbrella. The cave was not high enough for him to stand straight. Soon he calmed down again.

"Tell him," he said, "that I intend to go back to my own country as soon as I can find a ship. Tell him I would rather live in a cave with the gypsies dancing and singing and keeping me up all night than in his house. Also say thank you for his trouble and the many toothbrushes he has bought me while I have lived here."

After Lewis had finished the letter, he read it back to Mr. Madruga. It read:

Dear Charlie,

I don't want to sit in the corner. I want to make some shoes. You won't let me look for work. I am going home to Spain to live in a cave and stay up all night. Thank you for the toothbrushes.

"Excellent!" said Mr. Madruga. "You have the English style. The Spanish style is also very pretty. Now put 'With many wishes for your continued good health, I am always your obedient servant,' and then I will sign my name."

"Could you just say 'goodbye'?" asked Lewis.

Mr. Madruga looked disappointed.

"I can't spell all those words," Lewis explained.

"In that case, yes. Put 'goodbye.' But in Spanish. *Adiós.* You can spell that?"

"Is this right?" asked Lewis, after thinking awhile.

"Of course," said Mr. Madruga. "But a little mark is required over the *o* for emphasis."

Then Mr. Madruga signed his name, which took almost two entire lines.

"Is that just one name?" asked Lewis.

"Yes. It is nice to have such a name. When I am melancholy, I say my name over to myself and sometimes I feel cheerful again. Emilio del Camino de Herrera de Santiago Martinez y Madruga."

The candle went out.

"Will you hand him the letter?" asked Lewis.

"No," replied Mr. Madruga. "I will leave the table after the soup. I will put the letter next to his plate. Then I will go to my room and wait until he has read it."

"Will you come to the park tomorrow?"

"If not tomorrow, then the next day. Then I will tell you the news. Who knows what will happen? I may be put out on the street like an old table. In that case, of course, I will defend myself with the umbrella!"

Lewis buried the remains of the candle in a pile of leaves at the back of the cave. He poked the mosquito book in a crack in the wall. He placed the paper bird on a little projecting shelf, where the wind could not blow it away.

"*Adiós*," Lewis said to Mr. Madruga.

"*Adiós, amigo*," replied Mr. Madruga.

After supper that evening, Miss Fitchlow told Lewis a story about an owl who chased a mouse all over the world, through jungles and cities, across deserts and mountains, flying, riding on the masts of ships, even hiding in freight cars.

"Why did the owl want that special mouse?" asked Lewis.

"He had an *idée fixe*," said Miss Fitchlow.

"What's that?" Lewis asked.

"An idea that a person, or a bird, can't get rid of," explained Miss Fitchlow. She said that by the time the owl had caught up with the mouse, the mouse had become a plump, smart, giant mouse, very strong in the legs because of all the running it had had to do to escape the owl.

"Then what happened?" asked Lewis.

"Nothing much," said Miss Fitchlow.

"Did he eat it?" Lewis asked.

"Did who eat what?" she asked.

"The owl eat the mouse?"

"The owl gave up mice and rats and became a vegetarian," said Miss Fitchlow.

"Why?"

"Discretion is the better part of valor," said Miss Fitchlow, "which means that if your dinner is bigger and tougher than you are, you'd better change your diet."

"Oh," said Lewis.

"I feel a cartwheel coming on," said Miss Fitchlow. "Make way!"

And with that, she did a double cartwheel across the living room floor.

4

Mr. Madruga was not in the park Tuesday or Wednesday or Thursday. At first, Lewis was very disappointed. Perhaps Mr. Madruga hadn't liked the letter Lewis had written for him. Perhaps he had just forgotten about him.

Of course, Charlie might have given him errands to do or might have made him read all the newspapers. Charlie might have decided he didn't want Mr. Madruga to go to the park anymore. Or else the old man might have found a ship to take him home. Perhaps he was, even now, drinking his chocolate in a café and watching people walk on the *ramblas*.

Still, Lewis had his cave.

Every afternoon, after he had checked the square to make sure Mr. Madruga was not there, Lewis went to the cave. Wednesday, he had seen another DeKay's snake near the entrance and had wondered if it was the same one he had seen his first day in the park.

Miss Fitchlow had been starchy about matches so he was unable to light the candle—not that he really needed it.

"Fire is sacred, my boy," Miss Fitchlow had said. "Like most sacred things, it tends to get easily out of hand."

Lewis had a good time in the cave, although he missed Mr. Madruga. He furnished it with a shoebox for interesting stones and bottle tops, a box of saltines in case he got hungry, along with several handfuls of nuts Miss Fitchlow had given him, and the blanket he had used for reading to the children on the service stairs. The bird was still on the ledge, although its paper feathers had wilted a little.

To pass the time, he read the booklet about mosquitoes in Delaware. He thought maybe he could use it for a report for the class.

He wondered if he could stand on his head without Miss Fitchlow there to catch him if he fell over. He smoothed out a place on the dirt floor of the cave and covered it with leaves. The first time he tried he fell on his face. The second time he managed to get himself up, his legs straight and pointed up at the cave's roof. Then he let himself down in sections like a telescope and assumed the lotus position, breathing deeply. After that he felt quite light-headed.

On Thursday a small dog wandered into the cave. It was extremely friendly and it ate a number of peanuts from Lewis's hand. On the dog's collar tag Lewis read: "My name is Myra. I belong to Mr. Klopper."

"Myra," said Lewis. The dog wagged her tail.

"I bet somebody is following you," Lewis said. "I bet you're not even supposed to be in the park."

Myra wagged her tail.

"Say something," said Lewis.

Myra gave a low bark.

"I can spell anything," Lewis said. "Even that!"

Myra barked again.

"R-o-o-f," Lewis spelled. "Don't you know any other words? You're not responsible, Myra, old dog. You shouldn't be allowed out without a keeper. Take a letter, Myra. Ready? 'Dear Mr. Klopper, you shouldn't smile at Myra when you want her to stop doing something like chewing up the rug. Just tell her. Also, don't wake her up in the middle of the night to ask her what she's thinking about. It will make her have stiff brains.'"

Myra jumped up and licked Lewis's chin.

"Calm yourself," Lewis said sternly.

Myra drifted away after she and Lewis had finished the peanuts. It was pleasant to have guests dropping in.

After Myra left, Lewis began to feel sad again thinking about Mr. Madruga and wondering where he was. He tried saying the old man's name over to himself, but he could only remember half of it.

He went home earlier that afternoon. He walked up the service stairs thinking that maybe he'd find Henry or Thomas or Betty Anne to read to, but he only found Henry sitting outside his own door with an apple core in one hand.

"You don't read to us anymore," Henry said reproachfully.

"I have other things to do than read to you all the time," Lewis said. "Anyhow, you ought to learn to read yourself."

137

"I can read," Henry said in a sulky voice. "But I want to hear about the monkey's paw."

"You have heard about that a thousand times," Lewis said. "Read it yourself."

"I'll get somebody else to read it to me," Henry said.

"You're just a silly little kid," said Lewis crossly. Henry popped the apple core in his mouth and made a face at Lewis.

Lewis ran up to his own floor.

"I want to hear about that monkey," yelled Henry.

Lewis leaned over the railing and looked down at Henry.

"I'll haunt you myself," he said.

Henry giggled.

"Feeling spindly?" asked Miss Fitchlow that evening.

Whatever that was, Lewis guessed it was the way he was feeling.

"Cheer up!" said Miss Fitchlow. "The worst is yet to come!" With that, she gave a loud horse laugh. Then she showed Lewis how to do a cartwheel.

After a few moments of cartwheeling, Lewis did feel better. He told Miss Fitchlow all about Delaware's mosquito problems.

"Mercy!" she exclaimed. "I had no idea!"

He felt even better.

To Lewis's surprise, the word *mosquito* turned up in Friday morning's spelling test. He got it right. Better yet, the teacher didn't mention that he had gotten it right.

His plan was to go straight to the park after school. If Mr. Madruga wasn't there, he would go home. He didn't feel like visiting the cave today.

But when he got to the square, he saw Mr. Madruga sitting on his old bench. It was drizzling a little and Mr. Madruga had opened his umbrella.

"Well, well, dear friend. I'm so glad you came," said the old man. "I was afraid you might have forgotten me or thought I had gone away."

"I came every day," said Lewis.

"I thought you would, despite some doubts," said Mr. Madruga. "You are a good friend. Now. Let me tell you the news. My letter—no!—*our* letter astonished Charlie. Even Preciosa was astonished. I put the letter next to his plate, just as I said. Then from my room, I heard much crying and shouting and then a long silence. Then I hear the footsteps, then little taps at the door. I open the door. They are standing there. They don't wish me to go, they say. It would make them too sad if I went back to Barcelona. What could I do? Of course, I said I would stay."

The old man stood up and began to pace back and forth excitedly.

"But now, the big event!" he cried. "Charlie has a friend who has an uncle who is also a shoemaker. I have a job! The old man who worked for the uncle has now gone back to Italy so now the uncle needs a new old man. I am the new old man! Splendid, no?"

"Yes," said Lewis.

"Monday, everything begins," said Mr. Madruga. "I must go home now to shine my shoes and brush my hat and press my suit. I wish to give you a gift for your great help. Take this umbrella which my father gave me. Note the carved handle. It is a Spanish dragon. It is said such dragons used to live in Catalonia. Who knows? Perhaps they once did."

Mr. Madruga held out the umbrella. Lewis took it and then shook Mr. Madruga's hand.

"Thanks," he said.

"Until we meet again," said Mr. Madruga. "*Hasta la vista!*"

"*Adiós*," said Lewis.

When he got home, he saw that there were two suitcases in the hall. A minute later his mother, his father, and Miss Fitchlow appeared. His mother kissed him and his father squeezed his shoulder.

"Are you all right?" asked his mother.

"All right!" exclaimed Miss Fitchlow. "Why, he is extraordinarily well coordinated, having managed some very difficult yoga exercises right off. He is also the best-informed person on Delaware mosquitoes I have ever met."

"Well!" said his father.

"Why, Lewis!" said his mother.

Then his father noticed the umbrella which Lewis had furled and was leaning on.

"Where did you get that?" asked his father.

"A friend of mine gave it to me," said Lewis.

"But it's almost twice as big as you are," said his mother.

"I'll get bigger," said Lewis.

"Right!" said Miss Fitchlow.

The Mountain

Charles Mungoshi

We started for the bus station at first cockcrow that morning. It was the time of the death of the moon and very dark along the mountain path that would take us through the old village, across the mountain to the bus station beyond. A distance of five miles, uphill most of the way.

The mountain lay directly in our path and was shaped like a question mark. I liked to think of our path as a question, marked by the mountain. It was a dangerous way, Chemai had said, but I said that it was the shortest and quickest if we were to catch the 5 a.m. bus. I could see that he did not like it but he said nothing more, to avoid an early quarrel.

We were the same age, although I bossed him because I was in Form Two while he had gone only as far as Standard Two. He had had to stop because his father, who didn't believe in school anyway, said he could not get the money to send Chemai to a boarding school. We had grown up together and had become great friends but now I tolerated him only for old time's sake and because there was no one within miles

143

who could be friends with me. Someone who had gone to school, I mean. So I let Chemai think we were still great friends although I found him tedious and I preferred to be alone most of the time, reading or dreaming. It is sad when you have grown up together but I could not help it. He knew so little and was afraid of so many things and talked and believed so much rot and superstition that I could not be his friend without catching his fever.

From home the path ran along the edge of a gully. It was a deep, steep gully but we knew our way. The gully was black now and in the darkness the path along its rim was whitish. You never know how much you notice things on a path: rocks, sticking-out roots of trees, holes, etc., until you walk that path at night. Then your feet grow eyes and you skirt and jump obstacles as easily as if it were broad daylight.

On our right, away into the distance, was bush and short grass and boulders and other smaller gullies and low hills that we could not see clearly. Ahead of us dawn was coming up beyond the mountain but it would be long, not till almost sunrise, before the people in the old village saw the light. The mountain cast a deep shadow over the village.

We walked along in silence but I knew Chemai was afraid all the time and very angry with me. He kept looking warily over his shoulder and stopping now and then to listen and say, "What's that?" although there was nothing. The night was perfectly still except for the cocks crowing behind us or way ahead of us in the old village. We barely made any noise in our rubber-soled canvas shoes. It can be irritating when someone you are walking with goes on talking when you don't want to—especially at night. There was nothing to be afraid of but he behaved as if there was. And then he began to talk about the Spirit of the Mountain.

He was talking of the legendary gold mine (although I didn't believe in it, really) that the Europeans had failed to drill on top of the mountain. The mountain had been the home of the ruling ancestors of this land and the gold was supposed to be theirs. No stranger could touch it, the people said. We had heard these things when we were children but Chemai told them as if I were a stranger, as if I knew nothing at all. And to annoy him, because he was annoying me, I said, "Oh, fibs. That's all lies."

He started as if I had said something I would be sorry for. "But there are the holes and shallow pits that they dug to prove it."

"Who dug?"

"The Europeans. They wanted to have the gold but the Spirit would not let them have it."

"They found no gold. That's why they left," I said.

"If you climb the mountain you will see the holes, the iron ropes and iron girders that they abandoned when the Spirit of the Mountain broke them and filled the holes with rocks as soon as they were dug."

"Who told you all this?" I asked. I knew no one ever went on top of that mountain—especially on that part of it where these things were supposed to be.

"All the people say so."

"They lie."

"Oh, what's wrong with you? You know it's true but just because you have been to school you think you know better."

I knew he was angry now. I said, "And don't I, though? All these things are just in your head. You like being afraid and you create all sorts of horrors to make your life exciting."

"Nobody has to listen to you. These things happen whether you say so or not."

"Nothing happens but fear in your head."

"Do you argue with me?" His voice had gathered fury.

"Remember I grew up here too," I said.

"But you haven't seen the things I have seen on that mountain."

"What have you seen?"

"Don't talk so loud." He lowered his voice and went on, "Sometimes you hear drums beating up there and cows lowing and the cattle-driving whistles of the herd boys. Sometimes early in the hot morning sun you see rice spread out to dry on the rocks. And you hear women laughing at a washing place on a river but you cannot see them."

"I don't believe it," I said. The darkness seemed to thicken and I could not see the path clearly. "I don't believe it," I said again and then I thought how funny it would be if the mountain suddenly broke into wild drumbeats now. It was crazy, of course, but for no apparent reason at all I remembered the childhood fear of pointing at a grave lest your hand got cut off.

It was silly, but walking at night is unnerving. I didn't mind it when I was a kid because I always had Father with me then. But when you are alone a bush may appear to move and you must stop to make sure it is only a bush. You are not quite sure of where you are at night. You see too many things and all of them dark so you don't know what these things are, for they have no voice. They will neither move nor talk and so you are afraid. It is then you want someone older, like Father, to take care of things for you. There are many things that must be left unsaid at night but Chemai kept on talking of them. Of course the teachers said this was all nonsense. I wished it were so easy to say so here as at school or in your heart as in your mouth. But it would not help us to show Chemai that I was frightened too. However, I had to shut him up.

"Can't you ever stop your yapping?"

We had crossed a sort of low hill and were dropping slightly but immediately we were climbing sharply toward the mountain. It loomed dark ahead of us like a sleeping animal. We could only see its jagged outline against the softening eastern sky. Chemai was walking so lightly that I constantly looked back to see if he was there. We walked in silence for some time but as I kept looking back to see whether he was there I asked him about the road that I had heard was going to be constructed across the mountain.

"They tried but they could not make it," he said.

"Why couldn't they?"

"Their instruments wouldn't work on the mountain."

"But I heard that the mountain was too steep and there were too many sharp, short turns."

"No. Their instruments filled up with water."

"But they are going to build it," I said. "They are going to make that road and then the drums are going to stop beating." He kept quiet and I went on talking. It was maddening. Now that I wanted to talk he kept quiet. I said, "As soon as they set straight what's bothering them they are going to make that road." I waited for him to answer but he didn't. I looked over my shoulder. Satisfied, I continued. "And think how nice and simple it's going to be when the road is made. A bus will be able to get to us in the village. Nobody will have to carry things on their heads to the station anymore. There will be a goods store and a butchery and everybody will get tea and sugar and your drums won't bother anyone. They shall be silenced forever."

Just as listening to someone talking can be trying, so talking to someone who, for all you know, may not be listening, can be tiring. I shut up angrily.

We left the bush and short grass and were now passing under some tall dark trees that touched above our heads. We

147

were on a stretch of level ground. We couldn't see the path here because there were so many dead leaves all over the ground and no broken grass to mark the way.

I couldn't say why but my tongue grew heavy in my mouth and there was a lightness in my head and a tingling in my belly. I could hear Chemai breathing lightly, with that lightness that is a great effort to suppress a scream; almost a catching of the breath as when you have just entered a room and you don't want anyone in the room to know that you are about.

Suddenly through the dark trees a warm wind hit us in the face as if someone had breathed on us. My belly tightened but I did not stop. I heard Chemai hold his breath and gasp, "We have just passed a witch." I wanted to scream at him to stop it but I had not the voice. Then we came out of the trees and were in the bush and short grass, climbing again. I released breath slowly. It was much lighter here, and cooler.

Much later, I said, "That was a bad place."

Chemai said, "That's where my father met witches eating human bones, riding on their husbands."

"Oh, you and your . . ." He had suddenly grabbed me by the arm. He said nothing. Instinctively I looked behind us.

There was a black goat following us.

I don't know why I laughed. Then after I had laughed I felt sick. I expected the sky to come shattering itself round my ears but nothing happened, except Chemai's fear-agitated hand on my shoulder.

"Why shouldn't I laugh?" I asked. "I'm not afraid of a goat."

Chemai held me tighter. He was shaking me as if he had paralysis agitans. I grew sicker. But I did not fall down. We pushed on, climbing now, not steeply, but enough to make us sweat, toward the old village, into the shadow of the mountain whose outline had now become sharper. It was lighter than

148

when we had started, probably third cockcrow, but it was still dark enough to make us sweat with fear.

"You have insulted her," Chemai said accusingly.

I said nothing. It was no use pretending I didn't know what I was doing. I knew these goats. Lost spirits. Because I had laughed at it it would follow me wherever I went. It would eat with me, bathe with me, sleep with me. It would behave in every way as if I were its friend or, better still, its husband. It was a goat in body but a human being in spirit. We had seen these goats, as children, grazing peacefully on the hills and there was nothing in them to tell they were wandering spirits. It wasn't until someone laughed at them or said something nasty to them that they would file in a most ungoatlike manner after whoever had insulted them. And then when this happened it needed the elders and much medicine brewing to appease them, to make them go away.

We walked on very quietly now. We came into the open near the old village school. The path would pass below the old church, and a mile or less on we would enter the village.

There would be no question of our proceeding beyond the village this morning, while it was still dark. I didn't care whether we caught the five o'clock bus or not. I just did not have the strength to cross the mountain before the sun came up.

Also I had to see my grandmother about our companion.

"Let's wait for daylight in the village," I told Chemai. I saw his head bob vigorously in the dark.

My grandmother lived in the old village. She had refused to accompany us and many other people of the village when we moved further west to be near water. She had said this was home—our home—and she would die here and be buried here and anyone who died in the family would be brought back to

149

the old village to be buried. She had had a long argument with my father but she had been firm.

I did not like the old village nor Grandmother Jape because both of them reminded me of my childhood and the many nightmares in which I dreamed of nothing but the mountain having moved and buried us under it. And then I would scream out and wake up and the first thing I would smell was Grandmother Jape's smoke-dyed, lice-infested blankets that were coarse and, warmly itchy and very uncomfortable to sleep in.

I rarely paid her any visits now, and I wouldn't have stopped to say hello were it not for the goat and my fear to cross the mountain in the dark. She would know what to do.

We were now below the church.

Suddenly the church gave me an idea. It had two doors each in opposite walls. We would try to leave the goat in the church. It was a further insult but I felt the risk was worth taking.

When I told Chemai he said he did not like it.

"I shall try it anyway," I said.

"She will not stay. She will get out."

We went up the path leading to the church door. We went in. The goat followed. I shouted, "To the other door, quick!"

Chemai rushed for the opposite door. The goat followed him but stopped suddenly when the door banged to in its face. I slipped through this other door and shut that one behind me too.

Free. We ran for the village a mile up the hill.

Grandmother's hut was near the centre of the village. I knew my way about and in a short time we were knocking on her door, each time looking back over our shoulders to see whether the goat had escaped. I had to say, "It's me, Nharo" before Grandmother would open for us. "Many things walk the night with evil in their hearts," she had once told me.

"What brings you here in the middle of the night?"

"Nothing. We are going to the bus. We want to go to Umtali."

"To the bus at this hour? Are you mad? You must be . . ." She was looking behind us and I knew our friend had escaped. Quickly we slipped through the door, but the goat followed us into the hut.

Without saying anything Grandmother was already busy with her medicine pots. And suddenly, safe and warm, I felt that the goat was harmless. It was just a wronged friend and would go away when paid. I looked at it. It was a small she-goat, spotless black. In the dim fireglow of Grandmother's hut it looked almost sad.

Grandmother was eating medicines and Chemai was watching her intently. I felt safe. Somebody who knew was taking care of things at last. It is a comforting feeling to have someone who knows take care of those things you don't know.

Afternoon in Linen

Shirley Jackson

It was a long, cool room, comfortably furnished and happily placed, with hydrangea bushes outside the large windows and their pleasant shadows on the floor. Everyone in it was wearing linen—the little girl in the pink linen dress with a wide blue belt, Mrs. Kator in a brown linen suit and a big, yellow linen hat, Mrs. Lennon, who was the little girl's grandmother, in a white linen dress, and Mrs. Kator's little boy, Howard, in a blue linen shirt and shorts. Like in *Alice Through the Looking-Glass*, the little girl thought, looking at her grandmother; like the gentleman all dressed in white paper. I'm a gentleman all dressed in pink paper, she thought. Although Mrs. Lennon and Mrs. Kator lived on the same block and saw each other every day, this was a formal call, and so they were drinking tea.

Howard was sitting at the piano at one end of the long room, in front of the biggest window. He was playing "Humoresque" in careful, unhurried tempo. I played that last year, the little girl thought; it's in G. Mrs. Lennon and Mrs. Kator were still holding their teacups, listening to Howard and looking at him,

153

and now and then looking at each other and smiling. I could still play that if I wanted to, the little girl thought.

When Howard had finished playing "Humoresque," he slid off the piano bench and came over and gravely sat down beside the little girl, waiting for his mother to tell him whether to play again or not. He's bigger than I am, she thought, but I'm older. I'm ten. If they ask me to play the piano for them now, I'll say no.

"I think you play very nicely, Howard," the little girl's grandmother said. There were a few moments of leaden silence. Then Mrs. Kator said, "Howard, Mrs. Lennon spoke to you." Howard murmured and looked at his hands on his knees.

"I think he's coming along very well," Mrs. Kator said to Mrs. Lennon. "He doesn't like to practice, but I think he's coming along well."

"Harriet loves to practice," the little girl's grandmother said. "She sits at the piano for hours, making up little tunes and singing."

"She probably has a real talent for music," Mrs. Kator said. "I often wonder whether Howard is getting as much out of his music as he should."

"Harriet," Mrs. Lennon said to the little girl, "won't you play for Mrs. Kator? Play one of your own little tunes."

"I don't know any," the little girl said.

"Of course you do, dear," her grandmother said.

"I'd like very much to hear a little tune you made up yourself, Harriet," Mrs. Kator said.

"I don't know any," the little girl said.

Mrs. Lennon looked at Mrs. Kator and shrugged. Mrs. Kator nodded, mouthing "Shy," and turned to look proudly at Howard.

The little girl's grandmother set her lips firmly in a tight, sweet smile. "Harriet dear," she said, "even if we don't want to play our little tunes, I think we ought to tell Mrs. Kator that music is not our forte. I think we ought to show her our really fine achievements in another line. Harriet," she continued, turning to Mrs. Kator, "has written some poems. I'm going to ask her to recite them to you, because I feel, even though I may be prejudiced"—she laughed modestly—"even though I probably *am* prejudiced, that they show real merit."

"Well, for heaven's sake!" Mrs. Kator said. She looked at Harriet, pleased. "Why, dear, I didn't know you could do anything like that! I'd really *love* to hear them."

"Recite one of your poems for Mrs. Kator, Harriet."

The little girl looked at her grandmother, at the sweet smile, and at Mrs. Kator, leaning forward, and at Howard, sitting with his mouth open and a great delight growing in his eyes. "Don't know any," she said.

"Harriet," her grandmother said, "even if you don't remember any of your poems, you have some written down. I'm sure Mrs. Kator won't mind if you read them to her."

The huge merriment that had been gradually taking hold of Howard suddenly overwhelmed him. "Poems," he said, doubling up with laughter on the couch. "Harriet writes poems." He'll tell all the kids on the block, the little girl thought.

"I do believe Howard's jealous," Mrs. Kator said.

"Aw," Howard said. "I wouldn't write a poem. Bet you couldn't make *me* write a poem if you *tried*."

"You couldn't make me, either," the little girl said. "That's all a lie about the poems."

There was a long silence. Then "Why, Harriet!" the little girl's grandmother said in a sad voice. "What a thing to say

155

about your grandmother!" Mrs. Kator said. "I think you'd better apologize, Harriet," the little girl's grandmother said. Mrs. Kator said, "Why, you certainly *had* better."

"I didn't do anything," the little girl muttered. "I'm sorry."

The grandmother's voice was stern. "Now bring your poems out and read them to Mrs. Kator."

"I don't have any, honestly, Grandma," the little girl said desperately. "Honestly, I don't have any of those poems."

"Well, *I* have," the grandmother said. "Bring them to me from the top desk drawer."

The little girl hesitated for a minute, watching her grandmother's straight mouth and frowning eyes.

"Howard will get them for you, Mrs. Lennon," Mrs. Kator said.

"Sure," Howard said. He jumped up and ran over to the desk, pulling open the drawer. "What do they look like?" he shouted.

"In an envelope," the grandmother said tightly. "In a brown envelope with 'Harriet's poetry' written on the front."

"Here it is," Howard said. He pulled some papers out of the envelope and studied them a moment. "Look," he said. "Harriet's poems—about stars." He ran to his mother, giggling and holding out the papers. "Look, Mother, Harriet's poetry's about stars!"

"Give them to Mrs. Lennon, dear," Howard's mother said. "It was very rude to open the envelope first."

Mrs. Lennon took the envelope and the papers and held them out to Harriet. "Will you read them or shall I?" she asked kindly. Harriet shook her head. The grandmother sighed at Mrs. Kator and took up the first sheet of paper. Mrs. Kator leaned forward eagerly and Howard settled down at her feet, hugging his knees and putting his face against his leg to keep from laughing. The grandmother cleared her throat, smiled at Harriet, and began to read.

" 'The Evening Star,' " she announced.

When evening shadows are falling,
And dark gathers closely around,
And all the night creatures are calling,
And the wind makes a lonesome sound,

I wait for the first star to come out,
And look for its silvery beams,
When the blue and green twilight is all about,
And grandly a lone star gleams.

Howard could contain himself no longer. "Harriet writes poems about stars!"

"Why, it's lovely, Harriet dear!" Mrs. Kator said. "I think it's really lovely, honestly. I don't see what you're so shy about it for."

"There, you see, Harriet?" Mrs. Lennon said. "Mrs. Kator thinks your poetry is very nice. Now aren't you sorry you made such a fuss about such a little thing?"

He'll tell all the kids on the block, Harriet thought. "I didn't write it," she said.

"Why, Harriet!" Her grandmother laughed. "You don't need to be so modest, child. You write very nice poems."

"I copied it out of a book," Harriet said. "I found it in a book and I copied it and gave it to my old grandmother and said I wrote it."

"I don't believe you'd do anything like that, Harriet," Mrs. Kator said, puzzled.

"I did *so*," Harriet maintained stubbornly. "I copied it right out of a book."

"Harriet, I don't believe you," her grandmother said.

Harriet looked at Howard, who was staring at her in admiration. "I copied it out of a book," she said to him. "I found the book in the library one day."

"I can't imagine her saying she did such a thing," Mrs. Lennon said to Mrs. Kator. Mrs. Kator shook her head.

"It was a book called"—Harriet thought a moment—"called *The Home Book of Verse*," she said. "That's what it was. And I copied every single word. I didn't make up *one*."

"Harriet, is this true?" her grandmother said. She turned to Mrs. Kator. "I'm afraid I must apologize for Harriet and for reading you the poem under false pretenses. I never dreamed she'd deceive me."

"Oh, they do," Mrs. Kator said deprecatingly. "They want attention and praise and sometimes they'll do almost anything. I'm sure Harriet didn't mean to be—well, dishonest."

"I did *so*," Harriet said. "I wanted everyone to think I wrote it. I said I wrote it on purpose." She went over and took the papers out of her grandmother's unresisting hand. "And you can't look at them anymore, either," she said, and held them in back of her, away from everyone.

THE MYSTERIES OF
THE CABALA

Isaac Bashevis Singer

Everyone knew us on Krochmalna Street. My friend Mendel and I walked there every day for hours, my hand on his shoulder, his on mine. We were so preoccupied telling each other stories that we stumbled into baskets of fruits and vegetables belonging to the market women, who shouted after us, "Are you blind or something, you slobs?"

I was ten or so. Mendel was already eleven. I was lean, white-skinned, with a scrawny neck, blue eyes, fiery red hair. My sidelocks were always flying as if in a wind; my gaberdine went unbuttoned, its pockets loaded with storybooks I rented two for a penny. Not only could I read a page of the Talmud by myself, I kept on trying my father's volumes of the Cabala, still without understanding much. On the end pages of these books I would draw, with colored pencils, six-winged angels, animals with two heads and with eyes in their tails, demons with horns, snouts, snakes' bodies, calves' feet. In the evening, when I stood on our balcony, I stared up into the star-studded sky and brooded about what there was before the creation of the world. At home everybody said I was growing up to be a crazy philosopher, like that professor in Germany who pondered and philosophized for years, until he arrived at the conclusion that a man should walk with his head down and his feet up.

My friend Mendel was the son of a coal porter. Every few weeks his father brought a huge basket of coal for our stoves, and my mother gave him a kopeck. Mendel was taller than I, dark like a gypsy, his hair so black it had a bluish tinge. He had a short nose, a chin with a split in the middle, and slanting eyes like a Tartar's. He wore a tattered gaberdine and torn boots. His family lived in one room at 13 Krochmalna Street. His mother, blind in one eye, dealt in crockery in a stall behind the markets.

We both had the same passion: inventing stories. We never got tired of listening to each other's tales. That late afternoon in summer, as we passed Yanash's bazaar, Mendel halted. He had a secret to tell me: it was not true his father was a coal porter. That was only a disguise. Actually he was richer than any Rothschild. His family had a palace in the forest, and another castle on the sea, full of gold, silver, and diamonds. I asked Mendel how they had become so rich, and he said, "Swear by your fringed garment you will never tell anyone."

I swore.

"Let's split a straw."

We picked up a straw and, each taking an end, tore it between us as a bond. In Mendel's Tartar eyes a dreamy smile appeared and he opened a mouth of extremely white teeth, just like a gypsy's. He said, "My father is a robber."

A shiver ran down my back. "Who does he rob?"

"He digs tunnels into banks and drags out their gold. He hides in the forest, waiting to ambush merchants. He wears a gun and a sword. He is a sorcerer, too, and he can enter the trunks of trees, even though no one can see any opening."

"So why does he have to be a porter?" I asked.

"So the police won't find out . . ."

Mendel told me that his father did not operate single-handed. He was the chief of twelve hundred thieves, whom he sent all over the world to rob people and bring back the booty. Some sailed the seas and attacked ships; others held up caravans in the desert. Mendel said that, besides his mother, his father had twelve concubines, captive princesses. And when he, Mendel, became bar mitzvah, he would also become a robber. He would marry a princess from the other side of the River Sambation. She was already waiting for Mendel to come to the palace and wed her. She had golden hair falling to her ankles and wore golden slippers on her feet. To keep her from running away, Mendel's father had bound her to a pillar with a chain.

"Why does she want to run away?" I asked.

"Because she is yearning for her mother."

I knew it was all lies and even realized which storybooks the different parts came from, but his story enchanted me all the same. We were standing near the fish market, where carp, pike, and chub swam in tubs of water. It was Thursday and women were buying fish for the Sabbath. A blind beggar wearing dark glasses, with a cottony gray beard, plucked chords on a mandolin as he sang a heart-rending song about the sinking of the *Titanic*. On his shoulder stood a parrot picking at its feathers with its beak. The beggar's wife, young and as agile as a dancer, collected alms in a tambourine. Over the Wola section, the sun was setting, larger than usual, as yellow as gold. Farther out lay a huge, sulphur-yellow cloud blazing like a fiery river upon a bed of glowing coals. It made me think of the River of Fire in Gehenna, where the wicked are punished.

163

Mendel and I, even though we were best friends, were also silently engaged in a struggle. He was envious of me because my father was a rabbi and because we lived in an apartment with two rooms, a kitchen, and a balcony. He was always trying to prove that he was the stronger, cleverer, and more learned one. Now I was trying to invent a story as wonderful as Mendel's, or even more so. Abruptly I said, "I also have a secret I've never told you."

Mendel's Tartar eyes filled with mockery. "What's your secret?"

"Swear you won't tell anyone."

Mendel swore with a false smile and a look that almost seemed to be winking at someone unseen.

I said: "I know the Cabala!"

Mendel's eyes narrowed into slits. "You? How could you know it?"

"My father taught it to me."

"Is it allowed—to teach a boy the Cabala?"

"I'm different from other boys."

"Well . . . ! So what did you learn?"

"I can create pigeons. I can make wine flow from the wall. I can recite a spell and fly up in the air."

"What else?"

"I can take seven-mile steps."

"What else?"

"I can turn invisible. And I can change pebbles into pearls."

Mendel began to twist one of his sidelocks. Just as mine were disheveled, his were twirled tightly like two little horns.

"If that's so, you could have more money than the richest man in the world."

"Yes. True."

"So why haven't you got it?"

"One is not allowed to make use of the Cabala. It's dangerous. There is one spell that if you utter it the sky turns red like fire, the sea begins to churn, and the waves rise until they touch the clouds. All the animals drown; all the buildings collapse; an abyss opens and the whole world becomes black as midnight."

"How does that spell go?"

"Do you want me to destroy the world?"

"Nnnn . . . no."

"When I'm older, I will get permission from the prophet Elijah to fly to the Holy Land. There I will live in a ruin and bring the Messiah."

Mendel bent his head. He picked up a piece of paper from the sidewalk and began to fold it into a bird. I expected him to ask many more questions, but he remained stubbornly silent. All at once I felt that in my ambition I had overdone it; it was Mendel's fault. He had driven me to try to make myself too great. My own words had frightened me. One is not allowed to play games with the Cabala. Terrible nightmares might invade my sleep. I said, "Mendel, I want to go home."

"Let's go."

We moved toward the gate that led to Mirowski Street, no longer walking with our arms about each other's shoulders, but a little apart. Instead of drawing us closer, our talk had separated us. But why? I suddenly noticed how ragged Mendel's clothes were. The toe of his left boot had opened like a mouth and the nails stuck up like teeth. We came out on Mirowski Street, which was littered with horse dung, straw off farmers' carts, rotten fruit thrown out by the fruit merchants. Between the two city streets stood a building where ice was manufactured. Though it was still day outside, inside the electric lights were burning. Wheels turned rapidly; leather conveyor belts flowed; signals lit up and extinguished themselves. Not a single person was to be seen. Uncanny noises came from in there. Under our feet, through grates, we could see into cellars where tanks full of water were turning to ice. For quite a while Mendel and I stood there gawking; then we moved on. I asked suddenly, "Who feeds her?"

Mendel seemed to wake up. "What are you talking about?"

"I mean the girl with the golden slippers."

"There are maidservants there."

Not far from the second market, I saw two coins, two copper six-groschen pieces that lay side by side as if someone had placed them on the sidewalk. I bent down and picked them up. Mendel, seeing them too, cried out, "Partners!"

I gave him one immediately, though at the same time I thought that if it had been he who had picked them up, he would not have given me one. Mendel looked at the coin from every angle and then he said, "If you can turn pebbles into pearls, what do you want a six-groschen for?"

I would have liked to ask him: And if your father is such a rich robber, what do *you* want a six-groschen for? But something held me back. I was suddenly aware how yellowish his skin was and what high cheekbones he had. Something in that face spoke to me, but what it was saying I couldn't grasp. The lobes of his ears were attached to his cheeks; the wings of his nostrils rose and fell like a horse's. The corners of his mouth curled with envy and his black eyes scorned me. He asked, "What are you going to buy with your money? Candy?"

"I will give it to charity," I answered.

"Here—here's a poor man."

In the middle of the sidewalk, on a board with little wheels, sat half a man; he looked as if he had been sawed across the middle. Both hands gripped pieces of wood padded with cloth, on which he leaned. He wore his cap visor over his eyes, and a torn jacket. On his neck hung a cup to throw alms in. I knew very well what could be bought for six-groschen—colored pencils, storybooks, halvah—but some pride ordered me not to hesitate. Stretching my arm out, I tossed the coin in the cup. The cripple, as if afraid I might change my mind and ask for it back, rolled away so quickly that he almost knocked somebody over.

Mendel's eyebrows came together. "When do you study the Cabala? At night?"

"After midnight."

"So what's going on in heaven?"

I lifted my eyes to the sky and it was red, with black and blue streaks across the middle, as if a storm were coming. Two birds flapped up, screeching, calling each other. The moon had come out. Only a minute ago it had been day. Now night had fallen. The women at the street stands were cleaning up their merchandise. A man with a long stick was walking from one lamppost to the next, lighting the gas flames. I wanted to answer Mendel but couldn't think what to say. I was ashamed of my pretending, as though I were suddenly a grownup. I said, "Mendel, enough of these lies."

"What's the matter, huh?"

"I don't study the Cabala and your father is not a robber."

Mendel stopped. "Why are you so angry? Because you gave your six-groschen to the beggar?"

"I'm not angry. If you have a palace in the forest, you don't carry coals all day long for Haim Leib. And you haven't got a girl with golden slippers. It's all a fairy story."

"So you want to quarrel? Don't think just because your father is a rabbi I'm going to flatter you. Maybe I have lied, but you'll never know the truth."

"What is there to know? You made it all up."

"I'll become a bandit, a real one."

"They will roast you in Gehenna."

"Let them roast me. I'm in love!"

I looked at him, shocked. "You're lying again."

"No, it's the truth. If not, may God strike me dead on the spot."

I knew Mendel would not swear such an oath in vain. I felt cold, as if someone with icy fingers had touched my ribs. "With a girl?"

"What else? With a boy? She lives in our courtyard. We'll get engaged. We'll go to my brother's in America."

"Aren't you ashamed . . . ?"

"Jacob also was in love. He kissed Rachel. It is written in the Bible."

"Girl chaser!"

And I began to run. Mendel screamed something after me and I even imagined that he was pursuing me. I ran until I reached the Radzymin study house. Near the door Mendel's father was praying, a tall, lean man with a sharp Adam's apple, a bent back, and a face that was coal black, like a chimney sweep's. His loins were girded with a rope. He shook, leaned forward, and beat his chest. I imagined he must be asking God's forgiveness for the blasphemies of his son.

At the east wall stood my father in a velvet gaberdine, wearing a broad-brimmed hat and a white sash about his waist. His head touched the wall as he swayed back and forth. A single candle burned in the menorah. No, I did not yet know the Cabala. But I knew that everything that was happening to me tonight was filled with its mysteries. I felt a deep sadness such as I had never felt before. When my father finished praying, I walked over to him and said, "Papa, I have to talk to you."

At my serious tone, my father looked at me out of his blue eyes. "What's the matter?"

"Papa, I want you to teach me the Cabala."

"So that's it? At your age it is forbidden to study the Cabala. It is written that these mysteries should not be divulged to a man before he is thirty."

"Papa, I want it now."

My father clutched his red beard. "What's your hurry? You can be a decent man without the Cabala."

"Papa, can one destroy the world with a holy spell?"

"The ancient saints could do everything. We can do nothing. Come, let's go home."

We moved toward the gate, where Rebecca, the baker's daughter, stood with baskets full of fresh rolls, bread, bagels warm from the oven. Women were picking over the baked goods and their crusts crackled. My father and I walked out into the street, where the gas lamps cast a yellow glow. Between two chimneys spouting smoke and sparks hung a large, blood-red moon.

"Is it true that people live there?" I asked.

My father was silent for a while. "What makes you think so? Nothing is known. Cabala is only for strong brains. When weak little brains are immersed in the Cabala—one can easily fall into insanity."

My father's words frightened me. I felt myself close to madness.

He said, "You are still a boy. When, God willing, you grow up, get married, have more sense, then you will find out what you can do."

"I'm not going to get married."

"What else? Stay a bachelor? It is written: 'He created it not in vain. He formed it to be inhabited.' You will grow up, be matched with a girl, and get engaged."

"What girl?"

"Who can know in advance?"

At that moment I realized why I was so sad. The street was full of girls but I didn't know who was going to be my betrothed. She, the one destined for me, didn't know either. It could be that we both bought candy in the same store, that we passed each other, looked at each other, not knowing that we were going to be man and wife. I began to look among the crowd. The street was full of girls my age, some a little younger, some older. One walked and licked an ice-cream cone. Another one nibbled cheesecake at Esther's candy store, holding it between her thumb and middle finger, with her pinky lifted up elegantly. A girl carrying books and notebooks under her arm, with red ribbons in her braids, a pleated skirt, and a black apron, had black-stockinged legs that looked like a doll's. The streets were full of the aroma of fresh bagels, of breezes coming from the Vistula and the Praga forest. Around the street lamps a myriad of winged creatures—moths, butterflies, gnats—whirled, deceived by the light into believing night was day. I looked at the upper floors, where girls stood on balconies, gazed out of windows. They were talking, singing, laughing. I listened to the noise of sewing machines, to a gramophone playing. Behind a window I saw the dark shadow of a girl. I imagined she was staring at me through the mesh of the curtain. I said to my father, "Papa, can you find out from the Cabala who you are going to get engaged to?"

My father stopped. "What do you have to know for? They know in heaven and that is enough."

For a while we walked in silence. Then my father asked, "Son, what has happened to you?"

All the lampposts became bent and all the lights foggy as my eyes filled with tears. "Papa, I don't know."

"You are growing up, my son. That is what is happening to you."

And my father suddenly did something he had never done before: he bent down and kissed my forehead.

READING NONFICTION

Some nonfiction texts, like autobiographies or accounts of historical events, can read like stories. Others, like instruction manuals and some textbooks, are written purely to give information. In the Great Books Roundtable program, you will be reading nonfiction texts that include both narrative (story) and informational parts and that also raise questions for discussion.

Below are some questions you can ask yourself to help you better understand a nonfiction selection and discover issues you want to discuss. Try asking yourself these questions after your first reading of the text. Then, after rereading, consider how your answers have changed.

The reading strategies on pages xxii–xxiii are also helpful when reading nonfiction.

SUGGESTED QUESTIONS FOR NONFICTION

- How would you describe the author's tone?
- To whom does the author seem to be speaking?
- What is the author's attitude toward his or her subject?
- What is the structure of the text—is it like a list, a story, a persuasive essay, or something else? What is the effect of putting it together this way?
- What is the author trying to make you think, feel, or believe?
- Is the author asking you to take some kind of action?

RATTLESNAKES

John Muir

There are many snakes in the canyons and lower forests, but they are mostly handsome and harmless. Of all the tourists and travelers who have visited Yosemite and the adjacent mountains, not one has been bitten by a snake of any sort, while thousands have been charmed by them. Some of them vie with the lizards in beauty of color and dress patterns. Only the rattlesnake is venomous, and he carefully keeps his venom to himself as far as man is concerned, unless his life is threatened.

Before I learned to respect rattlesnakes I killed two, the first on the San Joaquin plain. He was coiled comfortably around a tuft of bunch grass, and I discovered him when he was between my feet as I was stepping over him. He held his head down and did not attempt to strike, although in danger of being trampled. At that time, thirty years ago, I imagined that rattlesnakes should be killed wherever found. I had no weapon of any sort, and on the smooth plain there was not a stick or a stone within miles, so I crushed him by jumping on him, as the deer are said to do. Looking me in the face he saw

I meant mischief and quickly cast himself into a coil, ready to strike in defense. I knew he could not strike when traveling, therefore I threw handfuls of dirt and grass sods at him to tease him out of coil. He held his ground a few minutes, threatening and striking, and then started off to get rid of me. I ran forward and jumped on him, but he drew back his head so quickly my heel missed, and he also missed his stroke at me. Persecuted, tormented, again and again he tried to get away, bravely striking out to protect himself, but at last my heel came squarely down, sorely wounding him, and a few more brutal stampings crushed him. I felt degraded by the killing business, farther from heaven, and I made up my mind to try to be at least as fair and charitable as the snakes themselves and to kill no more save in self-defense.

The second killing might also, I think, have been avoided, and I have always felt somewhat sore and guilty about it. I had built a little cabin in Yosemite and for convenience in getting water, and for the sake of music and society, I led a small stream from Yosemite Creek into it. Running along the side of the wall it was not in the way, and it had just fall enough to ripple and sing in low, sweet tones, making delightful company, especially at night when I was lying awake. Then a few frogs came in and made merry with the stream—and one snake, I suppose to catch the frogs.

Returning from my long walks, I usually brought home a large handful of plants, partly for study, partly for ornament, and set them in a corner of the cabin, with their stems in the stream to keep them fresh. One day, when I picked up a handful that had begun to fade, I uncovered a large coiled rattler that had been hiding behind the flowers. Thus suddenly brought to light face-to-face with the rightful owner of the place, the poor reptile was desperately embarrassed, evidently realizing that he had no right in the cabin. It was not only fear that he showed, but a good deal of downright bashfulness and embarrassment, like that of a more than half-honest person caught under suspicious circumstances behind a door. Instead of striking or threatening to strike, though coiled and ready, he slowly drew his head down as far as he could, with awkward, confused kinks in his neck and a shamefaced expression, as if wishing the ground would open and hide him. I have looked into the eyes of so many wild animals that I feel sure I did not mistake the feelings of this unfortunate snake. I did not want to kill him, but I had many visitors, some of them children, and I oftentimes came in late at night, so I judged he must die.

Since then I have seen perhaps a hundred or more in these mountains, but I have never intentionally disturbed them, nor have they disturbed me to any great extent, even by accident, though in danger of being stepped on. Once, while I was on my knees kindling a fire, one glided under the arch made by my arm. He was only going away from the ground I had selected for a camp, and there was not the slightest danger, because I kept still and allowed him to go in peace. The only time I felt myself in serious danger was when I was coming out of the Tuolumne Canyon by a steep side canyon toward the head of Yosemite Creek. On an earthquake talus, a boulder in my way presented a front so high that I could just reach the upper edge of it while standing on the next below it. Drawing myself up, as soon as my head was above the flat top of it I caught sight of a coiled rattler. My hands had alarmed him, and he was ready for me, but even with this provocation, and when my head came in sight within a foot of him, he did not strike. The last time I sauntered through the big canyon I saw about two a day. One was not coiled, but neatly folded in a narrow space between two cobblestones on the side of the river, his head below the level of them, ready to shoot up like a jack-in-the-box for frogs or birds. My foot spanned the space above within an inch or two of his head, but he only held it lower. In making my way through a particularly tedious tangle of buckthorn, I parted the branches on the side of an open spot and threw my bundle of bread into it, and when with my arms free I was pushing through after it, I saw a small rattlesnake dragging his tail from beneath my bundle. When he caught sight of me he eyed me angrily, and with an air of righteous indignation seemed to be asking why I had thrown that stuff on him. He was so small that I was inclined to slight him, but he struck out so angrily that I drew back and approached the opening from the other side. But he had been listening, and when I looked through the brush I found him confronting me, still with a come-in-if-you-dare expression. In vain I tried to explain that I only wanted my bread; he stoutly held the ground in front of it, so I went back a dozen rods and kept still for half an hour, and when I returned he had gone.

One evening, near sundown, in a very rough, boulder-choked portion of the canyon, I searched long for a level spot for a bed and at last was glad to find a patch of flood-sand on the riverbank and a lot of driftwood close by for a campfire. But when I threw down my bundle, I found two snakes in possession of the ground. I might have passed the night even in this snake den without danger, for I never knew a single instance of their coming into camp in the night, but fearing that in so small a space some latecomers not aware of my presence might get stepped on when I was replenishing the fire, to avoid possible crowding I encamped on one of the earthquake boulders.

There are two species of *Crotalus* in the park, and when I was exploring the basin of Yosemite Creek I thought I had

178

discovered a new one. I saw a snake with curious divided appendages on its head. Going nearer, I found that the strange headgear was only the feet of a frog. Cutting a switch, I struck the snake lightly until he disgorged the poor frog, or rather allowed it to back out. On its return to the light from one of the very darkest of death valleys, it blinked a moment with a sort of dazed look, then plunged into a stream, apparently happy and well.

THROWING SNOWBALLS

Annie Dillard

Some boys taught me to play football. This was fine sport. You thought up a new strategy for every play and whispered it to the others. You went out for a pass, fooling everyone. Best, you got to throw yourself mightily at someone's running legs. Either you brought him down or you hit the ground flat out on your chin, with your arms empty before you. It was all or nothing. If you hesitated in fear, you would miss and get hurt: you would take a hard fall while the kid got away, or you would get kicked in the face while the kid got away. But if you flung yourself wholeheartedly at the back of his knees—if you gathered and joined body and soul and pointed them diving fearlessly—then you likely wouldn't get hurt, and you'd stop the ball. Your fate, and your team's score, depended on your concentration and courage. Nothing girls did could compare with it.

Boys welcomed me at baseball, too, for I had, through enthusiastic practice, what was weirdly known as a boy's arm. In winter, in the snow, there was neither baseball nor football, so the boys and I threw snowballs at passing cars. I got in

181

trouble throwing snowballs, and have seldom been happier since.

On one weekday morning after Christmas, six inches of new snow had just fallen. We were standing up to our boot tops in snow on a front yard on trafficked Reynolds Street, waiting for cars. The cars traveled Reynolds Street slowly and evenly; they were targets all but wrapped in red ribbons, cream puffs. We couldn't miss.

I was seven; the boys were eight, nine, and ten. The oldest two Fahey boys were there—Mikey and Peter—polite blond boys who lived near me on Lloyd Street, and who already had four brothers and sisters. My parents approved Mikey and Peter Fahey. Chickie McBride was there, a tough kid, and Billy Paul and Mackie Kean too, from across Reynolds, where the boys grew up dark and furious, grew up skinny, knowing, and skilled. We had all drifted from our houses that morning looking for action, and had found it here on Reynolds Street.

It was cloudy but cold. The cars' tires laid behind them on the snowy street a complex trail of beige chunks like crenelated castle walls. I had stepped on some earlier; they squeaked. We could have wished for more traffic. When a car came, we all popped it one. In the intervals between cars we reverted to the natural solitude of children.

I started making an iceball—a perfect iceball, from perfectly white snow, perfectly spherical, and squeezed perfectly translucent so no snow remained all the way through. (The Fahey boys and I considered it unfair actually to throw an iceball at somebody, but it had been known to happen.)

I had just embarked on the iceball project when we heard tire chains come clanking from afar. A black Buick was moving toward us down the street. We all spread out, banged together some regular snowballs, took aim, and, when the Buick drew nigh, fired.

A soft snowball hit the driver's windshield right before the driver's face. It made a smashed star with a hump in the middle.

Often, of course, we hit our target, but this time, the only time in all of life, the car pulled over and stopped. Its wide black door opened; a man got out of it, running. He didn't even close the car door.

He ran after us, and we ran away from him, up the snowy Reynolds sidewalk. At the corner, I looked back; incredibly, he was still after us. He was in city clothes: a suit and tie, street shoes. Any normal adult would have quit, having sprung us into flight and made his point. This man was gaining on us. He was a thin man, all action. All of a sudden, we were running for our lives.

Wordless, we split up. We were on our turf; we could lose ourselves in the neighborhood backyards, everyone for himself. I paused and considered. Everyone had vanished except Mikey Fahey, who was just rounding the corner of a yellow brick house. Poor Mikey, I trailed him. The driver of the Buick sensibly picked the two of us to follow. The man apparently had all day.

He chased Mikey and me around the yellow house and up a backyard path we knew by heart: under a low tree, up a bank, through a hedge, down some snowy steps, and across the grocery store's delivery driveway. We smashed through a gap in another hedge, entered a scruffy backyard, and ran around its back porch and tight between houses to Edgerton Avenue; we ran across Edgerton to an alley and up our own sliding woodpile to the Halls' front yard; he kept coming. We ran up Lloyd Street and wound through mazy backyards toward the steep hilltop at Willard and Lang.

He chased us silently, block after block. He chased us silently over picket fences, through thorny hedges, between houses, around garbage cans, and across streets. Every time I glanced back, choking for breath, I expected he would have quit. He must have been as breathless as we were. His jacket strained over his body. It was an immense discovery, pounding into my hot head with every sliding, joyous step, that this ordinary adult evidently knew what I thought only children who trained at football knew: that you have to fling yourself at what you're doing, you have to point yourself, forget yourself, aim, dive.

Mikey and I had nowhere to go, in our own neighborhood or out of it, but away from this man who was chasing us. He impelled us forward; we compelled him to follow our route. The air was cold; every breath tore my throat. We kept running, block after block; we kept improvising, backyard after backyard, running a frantic course and choosing it simultaneously, failing always to find small places or hard places to slow him down, and discovering always, exhilarated, dismayed, that only bare speed could save us—for he would never give up, this man—and we were losing speed.

He chased us through the backyard labyrinths of ten blocks before he caught us by our jackets. He caught us and we all stopped.

We three stood staggering, half blinded, coughing, in an obscure hilltop backyard: a man in his twenties, a boy, a girl. He had released our jackets, our pursuer, our captor, our hero: he knew we weren't going anywhere. We all played by the rules. Mikey and I unzipped our jackets. I pulled off my sopping mittens. Our tracks multiplied in the backyard's new snow. We had been breaking new snow all morning. We didn't look at each other. I was cherishing my excitement. The man's lower pants legs were wet; his cuffs were full of snow, and there was a prow of snow beneath them on his shoes and socks. Some trees bordered the little flat backyard, some messy winter trees. There was no one around: a clearing in a grove, and we the only players.

It was a long time before he could speak. I had some difficulty at first recalling why we were there. My lips felt swollen; I couldn't see out of the sides of my eyes; I kept coughing.

"You stupid kids," he began perfunctorily.

We listened perfunctorily indeed, if we listened at all, for the chewing out was redundant, a mere formality, and beside the point. The point was that he had chased us passionately without giving up, and so he had caught us. Now he came down to earth. I wanted the glory to last forever.

But how could the glory have lasted forever? We could have run through every backyard in North America until we got to Panama. But when he trapped us at the lip of the Panama Canal, what precisely could he have done to prolong the drama of the chase and cap its glory? I brooded about this for the next few years. He could only have fried Mikey Fahey and me in boiling oil, say, or dismembered us piecemeal, or staked us to anthills. None of which I really wanted, and none of which any adult was likely to do, even in the spirit of fun. He could only chew us out there in the Panamanian jungle, after months or years of exalting pursuit. He could only begin, "You stupid kids," and continue in his ordinary Pittsburgh accent with his normal righteous anger and the usual common sense.

If in that snowy backyard the driver of the black Buick had cut off our heads, Mikey's and mine, I would have died happy, for nothing has required so much of me since as being chased all over Pittsburgh in the middle of winter—running terrified, exhausted—by this sainted, skinny, furious redheaded man who wished to have a word with us. I don't know how he found his way back to his car.

READING POETRY

If you are puzzled about what to make of a poem, you are not alone. Poems are meant to be read over and over and discovered slowly. Asking questions about a poem can help you uncover more of its meaning and think about it in new ways.

Below are some questions you can ask yourself to help you better understand a poem and discover issues you want to discuss. Try asking yourself these questions after you read the poem once or twice. Then, after a couple more readings, consider how your answers have changed.

SUGGESTED QUESTIONS FOR POETRY

About the Poem and the Audience

- Who is the poem's speaker?
- What situation or event is happening?
- Who or what is the audience?
- How does the title relate to the rest of the poem?
- Does the poem have to do with a particular moment in history?
- Does the poem have to do with a particular culture or society?

About Poetic Language and Form

- ◆ What kind of form does the poem have? How does it look on the page?

- ◆ Does the poem use words in an unusual way?

- ◆ Is the way the words sound (not just what they mean) an important element of the poem?

- ◆ Does the poem use images to make the reader feel a certain way?

- ◆ What is the tone? How do you know?

WAYS TO READ POETRY

Below are some ways to read and mark a poem that can help you further explore the author's choice of rhythm, language, and structure.

Recognize Rhythm

- ◆ With a partner, take turns reading the poem aloud several times. Experiment with each reading by exaggerating the syllables of words, speeding up or slowing down your reading, or clapping out the poem's rhythm while you read.

- ◆ Read the poem as a whole class, clapping, stomping, or walking in time to the poem's rhythm as you read.

Listen to Language

- ◆ With a partner, take turns reading the poem aloud several times. Experiment with each reading by exaggerating your mouth movements, stressing the consonants or vowels of certain words, or communicating with your voice how certain words make you feel.

- Underline some of the poem's repeated sounds or letters. Reread the poem aloud, stressing the repetitions you underlined.

See the Structure

- Trace the end of each line of the poem with a pencil (as if connecting dots) to see what pattern the poem makes on the page.
- Read the poem aloud, taking a breath or pausing at the end of each *sentence* in the poem—wherever there is a period, question mark, or exclamation point. Then read the poem again, taking a breath or pausing at each *line break*—wherever the author stops a line. Compare the two readings. How were they different? How did each one make you feel about the poem? Did you notice anything new in either reading?

INTRODUCTION TO POETRY

Billy Collins

I ask them to take a poem
and hold it up to the light
like a color slide

or press an ear against its hive.

I say drop a mouse into a poem
and watch him probe his way out,

or walk inside the poem's room
and feel the walls for a light switch.

I want them to waterski
across the surface of a poem
waving at the author's name on the shore.

But all they want to do
is tie the poem to a chair with rope
and torture a confession out of it.

They begin beating it with a hose
to find out what it really means.

[I'M NOBODY! WHO ARE YOU?]

Emily Dickinson

I'm Nobody! Who are you?
Are you—Nobody—Too?
Then there's a pair of us!
Don't tell! they'd advertise—you know!

How dreary—to be—Somebody!
How public—like a Frog—
To tell one's name—the livelong June—
To an admiring Bog!

THIS IS JUST TO SAY

William Carlos Williams

I have eaten
the plums
that were in
the icebox

and which
you were probably
saving
for breakfast

Forgive me
they were delicious
so sweet
and so cold

MUSHROOMS

Sylvia Plath

Overnight, very
Whitely, discreetly,
Very quietly

Our toes, our noses
Take hold on the loam,
Acquire the air.

Nobody sees us,
Stops us, betrays us;
The small grains make room.

Soft fists insist on
Heaving the needles,
The leafy bedding,

Even the paving.
Our hammers, our rams,
Earless and eyeless,

Perfectly voiceless,
Widen the crannies,
Shoulder through holes. We

Diet on water,
On crumbs of shadow,
Bland-mannered, asking

Little or nothing.
So many of us!
So many of us!

We are shelves, we are
Tables, we are meek,
We are edible,

Nudgers and shovers
In spite of ourselves.
Our kind multiplies:

We shall by morning
Inherit the earth.
Our foot's in the door.

TABLE

Edip Cansever
Translated by Richard Tillinghast

A man filled with the gladness of living
Put his keys on the table,
Put flowers in a copper bowl there.
He put his eggs and milk on the table.
He put there the light that came in through the window,
Sound of a bicycle, sound of a spinning wheel.
The softness of bread and weather he put there.
On the table the man put
Things that happened in his mind.
What he wanted to do in life,
He put that there.
Those he loved, those he didn't love,
The man put them on the table too.
Three times three make nine:
The man put nine on the table.
He was next to the window next to the sky;
He reached out and placed on the table endlessness.
So many days he had wanted to drink a beer!
He put on the table the pouring of that beer.
He placed there his sleep and his wakefulness;
His hunger and his fullness he placed there.

Now that's what I call a table!
It didn't complain at all about the load.
It wobbled once or twice, then stood firm.
The man kept piling things on.

The Road Not Taken

Robert Frost

Two roads diverged in a yellow wood,
And sorry I could not travel both
And be one traveler, long I stood
And looked down one as far as I could
To where it bent in the undergrowth;

Then took the other, as just as fair,
And having perhaps the better claim,
Because it was grassy and wanted wear;
Though as for that the passing there
Had worn them really about the same,

And both that morning equally lay
In leaves no step had trodden black.
Oh, I kept the first for another day!
Yet knowing how way leads on to way,
I doubted if I should ever come back.

I shall be telling this with a sigh
Somewhere ages and ages hence:
Two roads diverged in a wood, and I—
I took the one less traveled by,
And that has made all the difference.

ACKNOWLEDGMENTS

Gaston, by William Saroyan. Copyright © 1962 by the Atlantic Monthly Company; renewed 1990 by the William Saroyan Foundation. Reprinted by permission of the Trustees of Leland Stanford Junior University.

The Old Man of the Sea, from THE SPRINGS OF AFFECTION: STORIES OF DUBLIN, by Maeve Brennan. Copyright © 1997 by The Estate of Maeve Brennan. Reprinted by permission of Houghton Mifflin Harcourt Publishing Company.

Through the Tunnel, from THE HABIT OF LOVING, by Doris Lessing. Copyright © 1957 by Doris Lessing. Originally published in the *New Yorker*, copyright © 1955 by Doris Lessing. Reprinted by permission of HarperCollins Publishers.

Raymond's Run, from GORILLA, MY LOVE, by Toni Cade Bambara. Copyright © 1971 by Toni Cade Bambara. Reprinted by permission of Random House, Inc.

The Witch Who Came for the Weekend, extract from JULIET'S STORY, by William Trevor. Copyright © 1991 by William Trevor. Reprinted by permission of PFD on behalf of William Trevor.

As the Night the Day, from MODERN AMERICAN PROSE, by Abioseh Nicol. Copyright © 1964 by Abioseh Nicol. Reprinted by permission of Harold Ober Associates, Inc.

The Parsley Garden, from THE ASSYRIAN AND OTHER STORIES, by William Saroyan. Copyright © 1949 by William Saroyan. Reprinted by permission of the Trustees of Leland Stanford Junior University.

The Veldt, by Ray Bradbury. Copyright © 1950 by the Curtis Publishing Company; renewed 1977 by Ray Bradbury. Reprinted by permission of Don Congdon Associates, Inc.

A Likely Place, by Paula Fox. Copyright © 1967 by Paula Fox. Reprinted by permission of Simon and Schuster Books for Young Readers, an imprint of Simon and Schuster Children's Publishing Division.

The Mountain, from THE SETTING SUN AND THE ROLLING WORLD, by Charles Mungoshi. Copyright © 1972, 1980 by Charles Mungoshi. Reprinted by permission of Beacon Press, Boston.

Afternoon in Linen, from THE LOTTERY AND OTHER STORIES, by Shirley Jackson. Copyright © 1948, 1949 by Shirley Jackson; renewed 1976, 1977 by Laurence Hyman, Barry Hyman, Mrs. Sarah Webster, and Mrs. Joanne Schnurer. Reprinted by permission of Farrar, Straus and Giroux, LLC.

ILLUSTRATION CREDITS